CAREER

MANAGEMENT TOOLKIT

for
job seekers
business owners
employers
& employees

by Brian Moore

ISBN: 978-0-646-52504-4

Original graphic design & layout by Carmel Glover

melisanda@optusnet.com.au

Redesigned by CasaDiAries

casadiaries@gmail.com

Formatted by Sushil & Shikha

ritzinfotek@gmail.com

To my amazing wife and best friend Jacinda for her unconditional love, support, patience and belief.

To my gorgeous children Samara, Jai and Yogi for making me so happy and so proud.

To my wonderful parents Patricia and Norman, for showing me what being a wonderful parent is all about.

Praise for the Career Management Toolkit

"The Career Management Toolkit is a high-quality toolkit that every professional should own."

It provides an easy-to-use framework and instruction set for individuals to plan for, and execute, a successful career or career shift. It covers the not-so common sense issues of how to write a good resume and cover letter; how to prepare for an interview and how to close the deal. It even covers what to do once you have that dream job. The toolkit captures and articulates the key learnings that take most professionals a lifetime to acquire.

LINDA DOWNS
ASIA PACIFIC HUMAN RESOURCES DIRECTOR, ERM (MALAYSIA)

"Whether you need to choose the right job or find the right job, the Career Management Toolkit has it all."

Everyone deserves to be in a job role that is satisfying and rewarding. Whether you are just starting out, or onto your third or fourth career change in a lifetime, Brian Moore's Career Management Toolkit will steer you in the right direction. This comprehensive guide shows you exactly how to design the job of your dreams, and how to get there. It covers what resources to use, how to stay on track and what to focus on to get the results you want. Whether you need to choose the right job or find the right job, the Career Management Toolkit has it all.

KRISHNA EVERSON
MARKETING MENTOR, HEALTH PRACTICE SUCCESS (AUSTRALIA)

"The 'Swiss army knife' of such guides - compact, practical and eminently useful."

MATTHEW MCGRATH
REGIONAL HEAD OF CORPORATE COMMUNICATIONS, ASIA PACIFIC (HONG KONG)

"The Career Management Toolkit gives an excellent insight into where you may be with your career and what your options might be."

If you are starting out or looking to make progress inside or outside of your organisation, the toolkit offers clear direction and poses important questions that will assist you.

It is an easy read and offers simple tips to guide you on your path to success.

SCOTT ARMSTRONG
GENERAL MANAGER GOLF, THE VINES RESORT AND COUNTRY CLUB (AUSTRALIA)

"I found the CMT filled with practical tips on finding, retaining and motivating staff."

I found it useful that the perspective of both the employee and employer was provided together. I think managers often neglect to consider both sides of the equation when considering either their own career planning or helping others plan theirs. Brian's real life examples were a clear illustration of these tips working. I will keep this as a reference in my HR planning.

ROBERT JOLLY
EXECUTIVE DIRECTOR, FERRIER HODGSON (INDONESIA)

"The Career Management Toolkit is a comprehensive guide for job seekers."

Important sessions in writing resumes and cover letters, attending interviews as well as searching for jobs are fully covered. Moreover, survival skills like time management and presentation are also on the list. I find the chapters on choosing the right job (the 10 Ps) and the right career are particularly good criteria when the critical decision is about to be made. In reading this Career Management Toolkit, you will appreciate that Brian is not only giving out career advice, but also tips on continuous self-improvement as needed in attaining one's career goal.

GLORIA KAM
AUSTRALIA

"I found the CMT most beneficial to both my business and personal life."

I run my own finance business and will be looking to employ my first staff member within the next 12 months, so from a potential employer's point of view, I now feel I'm in a much better position to do so. This material has provided me with tools to guide me towards the most suitable candidate.

I wish I'd had access to the CMT during my employed years, I think it would have made a vast difference to my life at that time. CMT is a brilliant tool for those working on choosing and getting the right job.

I also found the CMT very helpful from the perspective of my own self-development, specifically the time management, public speaking and self-marketing sessions. I am really happy to say that I have actively implemented positive changes to my business day as a direct result of my learnings. Thank you Brian for your inspiring work!

DIANE CLARKE
SENIOR FINANCE BROKER, LOANMARKET RESIDENTIAL AND COMMERCIAL FINANCE (AUSTRALIA)

"A highly recommended read and more than that, a key reference source!"

The Career Management Toolkit is precisely what the book title says it is - a 'toolkit' to help manage your career, and what a handy toolkit to have around. I have found myself referring to it often.

The CMT consolidates important information and advice into one convenient place (along with providing many new career insights) in a very sleek and readable package. The toolkit prompts you to ask critical questions which may have otherwise been overlooked.

The CMT is written in a very straightforward and readable format and once you start reading it, you'll want to read it cover to cover until you reach the end.

MITCHELL SCHOENBERG (CPA, CIA, CISA),
OPERATIONAL RISK MANAGEMENT CONSULTING - FREDDIE MAC, WASHINGTON, D.C. (USA)

"A very resourceful and comprehensive guide book for any keen career planner."

The Career Management Toolkit has been a guide book for my career planning. The 10 Ps provide insights in matching my personality and career objective in choosing my job. Writing a good and relevant resume to gain an interview, knowing the 'Do's' and 'Don'ts' at the interview, have got me successfully employed.

The Career Management Toolkit has become a quick reference guide for me whenever I encounter any challenges at work. Specifically, the 'quick guide to giving and receiving feedback', has enhanced my interpersonal communication skills with clients, colleagues and managers.

ALEX LIU
HONG KONG

"The CMT is a very good tool to review and keep you right on track."

Often in my career development, I have tended to jump from job to job with no real clarity or long term vision. I found the CMT helped me to focus on what I should be looking for, now and longer term. Using the kit, I was able to design a series of concise questions that I wanted to ask my next employer. I now feel more comfortable that I am in control of my future.

I particularly found the section on writing resumes & cover letters very informative. My resumes have been recycled and added to for the past 20 years. I have never really considered that it was outdated.

Following the CMT, I redesigned a concise, cohesive & structurally sound resume that will catch the eye of any employer. Using the 'AIDA' format that the CMT advises, I have been able to write a blistering cover letter that I feel certain will grab a potential employer's attention.

I was surprised to find a section on counter offers in the CMT. I recently resigned from a senior position with the company I worked for. Much to my surprise, my current employer made me a counter offer which threw me into some doubt and confusion. I was able to use the advice offered in the CMT to help clarify my thoughts and my next plan of action. I feel that this was timely advice considering my position.

Overall I was surprised at the depth and structure of the CMT. As a manager for the past 8 years, it's easy to slip into some poor habits without self reflection; particularly around managing staff performance, staff reviews and the like. Summarising the key points of the CMT in areas such as 'how to be a better public speaker' to 'using time management', and 'induction & feedback to employees', I realise that I have become a little lazy in my approach.

MATTHEW TIMOTHY MILLER
AUSTRALIA

"The Career Management Toolkit represents an essential aid to all of us eager to retain our place in the career value chain and to achieve the mantra of the author, 'Be your best, love your life!' "

Brian Moore is exceptionally qualified to present the fifteen chapters that break down within this toolkit. He has worked in major recruitment organisations across two continents and for many years has run his own professional practice. Like driving a car, the most effective learning is to assimilate knowledge into the consciousness, not even realising all the skill sets, information recall, analysis and execution necessary to bring everything together to perform the task. The Career Management Toolkit replicates that process as Brian reminds us, step by step, as to the vital elements of selecting, securing, promoting and realising our career goals. Much of these lessons reinforce grounded, practical sense rules that become so obvious after reading. Some of the anecdotes are both pitch perfect and strikingly simple i.e. 'in making public presentations, don't use humour unless you are funny'. So many presenters I have seen would have done well to remember such simple truths.

The lessons are not all proscriptive as Brian reminds, emphasises flexibility and illustrates that no one perfect style or format exists which would be equally appropriate for every case. But, these lessons serve to focus upon an objective and to improve the incidence of success for anyone who assimilates the wisdom imparted.

GRAHAME FARQUHAR
CFO, RESPONZE TV (USA)

"The Career Management Toolkit has provided me with valuable direction on how best to market and present myself within the public service."

Hi. My name is Michael. I am 43 years of age and consider myself a career public servant within the Federal Public Service. Recently I sought the assistance of a career planner, as I wanted to initiate some change within my career. My career planner referred me to a very valuable career management training resource. I am specifically referring to the Career Management Toolkit developed by Brian Moore.

Initially I was skeptical, as I have found most educational packages boring & repetitive in content. I have also considered my chances for career advancement within my department limited and unattainable. My decision to act on this referral has proven to be a very positive career move.

The Career Management Toolkit has provided me with valuable direction on how best to market and present myself within the public service. It has also helped me to carefully scrutinize what a particular job has to offer and whether it provides a challenging and rewarding career path. The toolkit has also helped me construct a more professional resume and fine tune many aspects of what career path I want to pursue. It has also helped me to identify personal and professional strengths that are relative to other government departments.

On a personal level, it has provided me with a career 'kick in the pants', and it has motivated me to seek the best possible results for myself and my family. I am thankful I took that advice. Recently I obtained a senior managerial position within a different government department, which presents greater challenges, responsibility and relocation interstate.

It is very clear Brian has an in-depth knowledge of career management and a passion for assisting people achieve their career goals. He has certainly assisted me in better planning my career and for that I am personally very appreciative.

MICHAEL NUGARA
AUSTRALIA

"The toolkit is an excellent, easy to read summary of best practice of the key areas covered."

The resume section is a good reminder and checklist for someone like myself, who has not been seeking new employment for some time.

BEN WILLIAMS
HONG KONG

Foreword

Brian has put together a practical guide, based on decades as a successful headhunter and career advisor. It could not be more timely, as millions struggle to find a new job in today's difficult markets, and as millions more look for the first real career post after school or university.

The contents are not gimmicky, or showy. They offer solid practical guidance, which, if followed, would certainly make an ordinary candidate look good, and a good candidate look perfect (recruiters always look for the perfect candidate, despite all life's experience telling them there is no such thing!).

There are useful sections on choosing the right career, and on choosing the right job. Good career management is like good marriage-making: finding those compatibilities which will make individual and employer happy with each other, growing together, and building each other's success. Material rewards usually follow, rather than lead, such mutual fit.

There are sections on self-marketing, and on preparing a CV or resume. Pitching at a new job with a new company is not easy. It requires confidence, or more, an aura of conviction which few amongst us find easy. Such confidence can of course be buttressed by a professionally structured CV tailored to the target job.

There are guidelines on making a success out of an interview opportunity, where Brian's expertise is particularly on show as he helps distil the essence of self-presentation, and how to assess the suitability of the potential employer and potential job. There is also a short section on how to respond to a counter-offer from the existing employer. Most careers develop with a move away from an employer, but many will see a return later to the earlier employer, or will lean on a reputation there, or at least will require a reasonable reference. For all these reasons, selling a departure to the current employer and parting amiably is sound practice.

Finally, Brian throws in for good measure, sections on public speaking and time management, and on inducting others, which are perhaps somewhat tangential to the main purpose, but represent a useful additional bonus!

ROGER HARRISON, *now retired, was formerly the Personnel Director of Unilever Australasia in the mid-nineties, and then the Senior Vice-President of the various Asia Unilever business groups. He was a lead player in laying the bedrock of the all-Asia Unilever region's ongoing success, through a storm of transformational appointments from top to bottom tiers of management in over thirty countries.*

TABLE OF CONTENTS

INTRODUCTION

Having spent the majority of my 20+ year working life in the recruitment industry, I have spent thousands of hours with thousands of people in very private 1 on 1 conversations. These conversations were generally based on 1 of 2 events – they were either a job seeker saying, "Brian, I want a new job and need your advice," or an employer saying, "Brian, I need you to find the perfect person for me for this vacancy."

I've also spent countless hours talking with both job seekers and employers about their lives in general, their career and life goals, and their continued pursuit of self-improvement.

The broad range of people I have advised over the years includes:

- Fresh school leavers and college graduates
- CEOs of large, medium and small companies
- Blue collar workers
- Defence personnel leaving the military
- Employees at all levels of seniority working for large, medium and small companies
- Government workers
- Scientists
- Stay-at-home mothers who are seeking to return work
- Retirees interested in re-entering the workforce

Having helped so many people towards achieving their career objectives and accumulating so much knowledge along the way about career management, I decided that it was time to take what I know and package it in such a way, so that I could help many millions of people around the world towards achieving their own career objectives and maybe even empower them to help others who they care about.

The Career Management Toolkit was created to provide you with valuable tools that you can constantly refer to throughout your life. Here are a few scenarios where you'll find **the Career Management Toolkit** invaluable:

- You are an employee who is seeking to improve your situation and prospects in your current company
- You are an employee who is seeking a new job

- You are unemployed and seeking a new job
- You are an employer who wants to improve the quality of people that you hire and be able to retain those people in your company
- You simply want to improve your own career management skills and those of the people that you care about

The Career Management Toolkit is great for parents who want to help guide the careers of their children, and also for educators, mentors, career coaches, business owners, and anyone interested in career success for themselves, their staff, their family and their friends.

The Career Management Toolkit contains 15 unique lessons which will help guide you throughout your entire career, both as an employee and as an employer. This is the key point of difference that makes **the Career Management Toolkit** so unique – it is a truly holistic approach to career management that you can continue to use throughout the whole of your working life, from the time that you leave school until the day that you retire. Regardless of where you fit into the companies that you work for, **the Career Management Toolkit** will help and encourage you to be your best.

The 15 lessons can be applied by you, whether you're a CEO or a fresh graduate, whether you work for a Fortune 500 company or a Government department, whether you're in the military or the not-for-profit industry, whether you're a stay-at-home mother or a retiree, eager to re-enter the workforce.

The investment you will make in **the Career Management Toolkit** will be repaid to you many times over throughout your career. I'm so pleased that you can now benefit from the many years of experience that I've enjoyed in advising and partnering with thousands of people in their pursuit of career satisfaction. I passionately believe that your investment in **the Career Management Toolkit** will bring you and those you care about, 'true peace of mind' and inspire you to enjoy the career happiness that you deserve.

Brian Moore

Brian Moore International Pte Ltd (BMI)
CareerManagementToolkit.com

twitter.com/better_career
facebook.com/careermanagementtoolkit

LESSON 01

The 10 Ps of choosing the right job

Life is full of difficult decisions. As residents of our own paradigms, we are constantly faced with making decisions in all aspects of our lives, decisions which will ultimately make either a positive or negative impact on us.

One important decision we all face at some point is accepting an offer of employment. We all want the perfect job but how do we know whether the job offer we're considering will in fact be the perfect job. Such answers are most often only found with the benefit of hindsight, sometimes with satisfaction, other times with regret.

Having recruited job seekers across many and varied functions, businesses and industries around the world since the early 1990s, I have seen both the successes and failures of choosing the right and wrong job. Many people have asked me if there is a formula for making the right choice, and I have always encouraged them to undertake as much due diligence as they possibly can before making their decision. In an attempt to help guide these job seekers to make the right decision, I consolidated the research I had performed through years of interviewing, and produced a set of guiding principles I call **'THE 10 Ps OF CHOOSING THE RIGHT JOB.'**

01 Position

What is the role and what do you think of it?

What does the company want you to do? Have they given you a job description and if so, is it clearly defined in terms of its objectives? The job description may set out the daily tasks, but have you been told what the company actually wants you to achieve? What are the key result areas and how will you know whether you're doing a good job? Will you be given the resources that you need to achieve your objectives?

What are the reporting lines both above and below you? Many people struggle with a widely used concept called Matrix Management, which presents you with more than one boss. You may have a functional line boss as well as a location boss and maybe even a business unit boss. The struggle comes when attempting to reach consensus on important decisions. If you haven't experienced this before, and are more used to quick and non-bureaucratic decision making, then you need to be aware of this challenge.

Ambiguity and lack of consensus can set you up to fail, simply because you won't know what doing a good job looks like.

Have you only been provided with a verbal job description? If you've been interviewed by multiple people, how many different versions of that verbal job description have you been given? Do you think everyone agrees on what your job will be? Do you have enough clarity on which to make an educated decision on whether to accept the role or not?

Ambiguity and lack of consensus can set you up to fail, simply because you won't know what doing a good job looks like. You don't want to be guessing - especially when your bonus compensation and promotional prospects depend on it.

Potential 02

Both for you and the company

I often advise people to not just think about the role on offer, but the next role as well. For example, the position on offer may be North American Head of a business, reporting to an International Head in an overseas head office. What will be your next step in 2-3 years? Your boss' job, requiring you to relocate overseas and travel globally?

What if you don't want to relocate? Can your role grow, can you take equity in the business, how will the company keep you inspired?

Also consider the company's potential. Is it in a 'sunset' industry with limited growth prospects? Is it in a regulated market which is to be deregulated? Is it a prime target to be taken over? Is the overseas parent committed to your region and markets?

03 Plan

What is the company's plan? Where are they heading?

Where is the company at, in terms of its evolution? Is it a mature company in a mature industry, happy to maintain the status quo? Is it a new company in a high growth phase? Is it a company which is downsizing or upsizing? Is it a company which is trying to re-invent itself? Is it a company destined for success or failure?

If you decide to accept an offer to join a company, you are committing the next phase of your career to that company, so you'll want to ensure that you're comfortable with what they have planned for the future. Is the company truly committed to what it's doing and plans to do, and how are they showing this?

Your role may or may not have a major influence on the company's plan and where it ends up heading. You may be the CEO with major influence, or you may be a functional or divisional head with limited influence, but you still want to have as clear a perspective as possible as to what the company plans to achieve. How can you plan to achieve if you don't know what the company plans to achieve?

People 04

What do you think of them?

As you've gone through the process of interviews and meetings with a company, you would have met a number of different people, in different positions, at different levels and maybe even different locations. With each person that you meet, you will gain an insight into the personality of the organisation and the chemistry amongst the staff members. You can then form an impression as to how you would fit in and get along with everyone.

Different impressions such as whether the people are passionate, gregarious, conservative, secretive, honest, friendly, collegial or individualistic, must be considered when you decide whether or not you want to spend all day every day with these people.

With each person that you meet, you will gain an insight into the personality of the organisation and the chemistry amongst the staff members.

You should always try to meet people who will be above, alongside and under you, to help form a more holistic impression of 'who' the company really is, or wants to be.

05 Product

Do you believe in their product/service?

Will you be proud to tell the world that you work for this company?

Will you be proud to tell the world that you work for this company? Do you think the company is destined for a successful future with what it has to offer? Do you or would you buy their products/services? Would you recommend them to friends and family?

Some people are against certain industries based on personal beliefs, whereas others don't care too much about what the company sells, so long as it's profitable, can afford to pay them and keep them employed.

Profile 06

...of your role, your division and the company (both internally & externally)

How visible will you be in the company, especially to the people who can influence your future? Is the role important enough to get you plenty of attention - whether you're doing a good or bad job? These questions relate both internally and externally. You may be scrutinised not only by peers, subordinates, your bosses and their bosses, but by the media, shareholders, competitors and the community at large.

What profile do you think your division has in the overall company? Is it seen as a growth oriented profit driver or a cash draining loss maker? Will this impact on how resources are made available to you and how much support you receive to achieve your objectives?

How visible will you be in the company, especially to the people who can influence your future?

How is the company perceived in the market? Is it a good corporate citizen and good employer? Is it a leader or a 'wannabe' in its industry? You can research this quite easily.

07 Package

Are you happy with it?
How flexible is it?

Is the base salary enough? When is it next reviewed? What bonus can you earn and how can you earn it? How much is based on your own performance compared with company performance? Will it be fully paid out annually or is a portion withheld for future years to stop you leaving? Do you receive your bonus in cash or is a portion converted to company shares? Is any of your bonus guaranteed? What are your tax and cost of living implications, should you need to relocate interstate or overseas? What other package benefits are on offer?

So many questions, but you need to be clear on the value of the package you're being offered and how it compares with what you're earning now. What will you leave on the table when you leave your current job and will any of that be absorbed by the new company?

What will you leave on the table when you leave your current job and will any of that be absorbed by the new company?

Place 08

Where is the job based? Are you happy about travelling?

How will you get to work? Is it convenient to get to? How long will it take? Do you need to relocate? How often will you need to travel and for how long? How much is this job going to keep you away from home?

These questions can relate to a new job either within your current jurisdiction, or requiring you to move to a new suburb/ state/country/continent.

How much is this job going to keep you away from home?

09 Public vs Private companies

This can impact on how the company makes decisions and your promotional prospects.

I have seen many people move from public companies to private companies and struggle, resulting in short and sometimes damaging tenures. Private companies often make both strategic and operational decisions quite differently from public companies, simply because the ultimate decision making power can sit with the owner of the company.

A CEO who owns the company can operate quite differently from a CEO who is merely an employee of a company, and this can frustrate many people who feel that they ultimately don't have any say - the CEO/Owner has absolute power.The board of directors may even be dominated by family members.

You need to think about how the company makes its decisions and who makes them.

I have also seen people struggle when moving from private to public companies, when they sense a diluted level of passion amongst senior management, due to their lack of ownership in the company. They feel that private company owners are much more passionate about the company's success because they own it and quite often, started the company themselves. They can also resent the media and shareholder scrutiny that often force public companies to act on short term strategies rather than longer term sustainable growth strategies.

When deciding whether to join a private or public company, you need to think about how the company makes it decisions and who makes them, as well as the most senior role you can expect to be promoted to in the future. Even in that most senior position, what impact will you have on overall strategic and operational decisions?

Price (Opportunity cost) 10

What impact will this job have on your life? What could you have missed out on by accepting this job?

This is the one 'P' that seldom gets enough attention when deciding whether or not to accept the offer of a new job. Having worked in the executive recruitment and career management industry since the early 1990s, there have been thousands of people who have confessed to me that they're in the wrong job, simply because of the negative impact it has had on their professional and personal life.

Long hours, frequent travel, unrealistic expectations, constant pressure, corrosive relationships - the list goes on as to what has caused the negative impact for the person, but the result is nearly always the same - they want a new job.

When questioned as to how they scrutinised the job offer initially in terms of 'opportunity cost', most admit they were more focused on many of the other 'Ps' than the ultimate price they might pay for accepting the offer. I continue to see people literally 'sell their souls' as they are tempted by the job rewards and not what it might cost. Many are satisfied with their choice, but many are not.

So, what is the desired result?

I call it the P that creates the freedom we all want... POWER!

You may ask why I haven't included Power as one of the 10 Ps. I believe that power is generated (at variable levels) through each of the 10 Ps. Power over how you go to and from work, what you do at work, how you succeed at work, how you balance your life with work, what you can do with the money you earn at work, the influence you have over others at work, the list goes on.

I'm not talking about power in a negative, ego driven and destructive sense, but the power that creates freedom and enlightenment. Freedom is one precious gift that I'm confident we all strive for.

Don't take any shortcuts with your decision; your happiness and freedom depend on it.

I recommend that you consider each of the 10 Ps to help you evaluate future job offers. See how your job offer holds up against each of the 10 Ps and you can then decide whether or not to accept the offer, based on an educated and informed decision. You may even want to consult your career advisor and go through the process with them. Your chance of complete success should then be much greater.

Don't take any shortcuts with your decision; your happiness and freedom depend on it.

I trust that 'The 10 Ps of Choosing the Right Job' will help guide you when you consider your next job offer. People continue to tell me that the 10 Ps has been their perfect sounding board for deciding 'yes' or 'no' on a new job offer, and I'm sure you'll feel the same, regardless of what job you're considering.

LESSON 02

How do you prepare a resume that gets the results you want?

Just about everyone in the workforce will at some stage in their career need to prepare a resume. Regardless of what level of job you have or how long you've been working, you will no doubt be asked for your resume by someone.

This lesson aims to provide you with the following information:

- The purpose of a resume in your search for a new role
- An outline of the content and detail which is necessary for an effective resume

Let's ask, what is the purpose of a resume?

A resume is your unique personal advertisement in the job market. You are in control of how it will look and what will be in it, so you should make the effort to get it right the first time. If you were writing any other advertisement, you would certainly concentrate on producing the best advertisement you were capable of.

This is the approach you should take with your resume, which can almost be the most important advertisement you will ever prepare. Your resume is your primary marketing tool in the job market and its number one objective is to secure you an interview. The document must attract the reader's attention, especially if the reader has received a large number of resumes in response to a job opportunity.

Your resume should provide relevant information about your career history, outlining to the reader why you are qualified and able to do the particular job you are applying for. The information you provide should be sufficient enough to persuade the reader to meet with you and provide an effective framework for your discussion.

Let's look at the next step: Preparing your resume

There is not one perfect format, outline or style for an effective resume. When comparing what is generally acceptable in various industries, you start to see how different, resume presentation can be. For instance, the investment banking industry tends to appreciate a 1 page resume from prospective candidates, whereas some government departments expect highly detailed submissions with supporting documents attached. Most industries expect resumes somewhere in between these 2 extremes.

Whilst much of this information about resume preparation may seem simple to some, many senior executives, especially those who may not have updated their resume for some time, find the task of writing an effective resume quite challenging. At the other end of the scale, college graduates need a great resume to help kick start their career, but many don't know where to start.

In terms of layout, the resume must be written in a 'reader friendly' format, consistent in its design and containing no typographical or grammatical errors, as attention to detail is highly regarded in all positions.

Do your best to avoid narrating your resume.Writing your career history as a story can frustrate the reader and risk your resume being pushed aside, so use bullet points to highlight your career experience instead.

Another golden rule to follow is to be honest. Don't exaggerate your experience or qualifications and don't exclude jobs that you may not

There is not one perfect format, outline or style for an effective resume.

have stayed at for very long. Let me tell you a brief story about a job candidate who made this error. This candidate first submitted a resume to me in 2000 and then sent an update in 2003. When reviewing the work career history, I compared the 2 resumes and in the 2003 edition, the candidate had left out a role that he had held for 4 months, even though he had included it in the 2000 edition. I made the candidate aware of his omission and advised that such dishonesty will do more damage than admitting that he had only spent 4 months in a role.

Trying to mislead the reader will in most cases come back to bite you.

Trying to mislead the reader will in most cases come back to bite you, as there are many ways to expose misrepresentations made in resumes eg; reference checks can expose this very easily and I have seen it happen - believe me, it's a very uncomfortable situation for all parties concerned, so it's better to be straight up from the start.

You should also be truthful about time gaps in your career history. Time spent unemployed should be included as exactly that, however you should be able to outline what you had done during this time off eg; travelling, further study, charity work, consulting.

If you are submitting your resume via the post, it is best to use high quality A4 paper. There is no hard and fast rule about what colour paper to use, so if you think that using blue paper will help your resume stand out from the crowd, then you should use blue paper, but of course plain white paper is the most generally accepted. Use a reader friendly font (size and design) and mark each page of a multi page resume with the page number and your name. Make sure to staple the document before you send it.

Some job seekers submit their resume on a disk, which can be a major headache for the reader if the document is saved in a format that the reader's computer doesn't accept. You may not receive a call from the reader asking you to resend your resume, so you are better off using paper in the first instance. There may be exceptions to the rule, such as in the advertising industry, where resumes, in the form of a portfolio of work are submitted on a disk.

If you, like most job seekers now, submit your resume electronically by email, then the format that you use, just like with submitting a resume on a disk, is very important. For example, different companies have different versions of Microsoft Word, which your version may or may not be compatible with. Emailing your resume in PDF format is a good idea as it adds a level of security to your document.

I also recommend not password protecting your electronic document as it simply makes the reader's job that little more difficult, and they may not have the patience. You must make the process as easy as possible for the reader. Remember that you want to be the first person they think of - for the right reasons.

Now, let's talk about resume components

Your resume should begin with a brief **summary/profile**, outlining the following:

- Your ideal role and areas of focus
- Key achievements that illustrate your success in similar roles
- Your key relevant areas of competence, which will transfer to the role you are applying for (remember that your competencies are your collection of skills, knowledge and attributes). Your skills can range from technical, financial, language, management, business development, leadership and negotiation

You want the reader to understand what you actually do in your role.

The main body of your resume is your **career history**. This history should start with your most recent role and you should remember to include the following:

- **Dates, including the month and year of each role**. Many senior executives don't include the month, but this omission will cause the reader to wonder whether the role was held from Jan '00 or Dec '00, which as you can see, leads to an almost 1 year discrepancy. Make sure you include the month

- **Company name, division, and a brief description of what the company does, especially if you feel that the company won't be easy recognisable to the reader.** I find that including the company's web address helps the reader enormously and shows initiative on your part

- **Position title, but make sure it will clearly identify what you do**. There are companies that invent creative titles for their staff, but to anyone outside that company, the title doesn't mean much. If you feel the title is confusing, you should immediately relate the title to a more widely used position title. I recently read a resume where the candidate's current title was Group Manager, but he failed to relate the title to the job function. After speaking with him, it was agreed that his title should have been Head of Project Finance

- **When listing your responsibilities, you should be aiming to illustrate the dimensions and purpose of your role, rather than listing every task that you are responsible for.** Include information such as what markets, people, budgets and products/services you are accountable for. In essence, you want the reader to understand what you actually do in your role (your mandate), not just your duties

- **The key content in your resume is the list of achievements in each of your career roles.** Your achievements show how you succeeded with the job description you were given when you started in the role - how you added value in your own unique way. Make sure you can state quantifiable facts and be specific

Whether the achievements relate to sales, profitability, headcount, new markets, new systems, new products/services or any other initiatives that you developed and implemented, you should be able to measure the achievement, so to give it more exact meaning that is easily understood. Quantitative measures are much less subjective than qualitative measures. The person reading your resume wants to know the facts. Try to be as positive as you can in your description.

No one has done exactly what you've done in your career.

After career history comes personal details, which should typically include:

- Full name, home address, telephone numbers, email address
- Citizenship (including whether you are a permanent resident of a country but a passport holder of another country)
- Language capabilities (spoken and written)
- Educational background: university qualifications both under-graduate and post-graduate. Include any specialist courses that your employers have sent you to, if you think they are meaningful and relevant. Only include your high school if you think it will add weight to your application
- Professional associations and memberships eg; CPA
- Hobbies & interests, but don't overdo it. Mention any clubs that you think may add weight to your application

As I mentioned at the beginning of this lesson, your resume is your unique personal advertisement in the job market. Keep in mind that you may need to tailor your resume to each company you send it to, depending on the role you are applying for. The CEO of a fast moving consumer goods company may apply for two CEO roles - one at a pharmaceutical company and one at a consumer bank. The CEO may be relevant for both companies but this will depend on how the resume is structured for each company, to highlight how the CEO's experience and competencies are relevant to each company.

Summary

In summary, take your time, think it through, and treat your resume with respect. No one has done exactly what you've done in your career, so your resume is your opportunity to show the world what makes you unique.

I trust that this lesson will help guide you when you next prepare your resume. When people think of their resume as their personal advertisement in the job market, they tend to take more time and care, and ultimately, pride in what they're producing. Your hit rate for gaining interviews should be much higher as a result.

LESSON 03

How do you prepare a cover letter that works?

Not everyone decides to include a cover letter when they submit their resume. There are all sorts of reasons for this, but for those who do, they should follow some golden rules when writing the letter.

A - Attention

Your cover letter should be a 'persuasive document' because its purpose is to entice the reader to show a further interest in what you're proposing. Quite simply, you want them to interview you.

There are 2 well known formats to follow when structuring a persuasive letter. One is the AIDA format, which stands for attention, interest, desire, action, and the other is the IDEA format, which stands for interest, desire, enthusiasm, action. Both aim to achieve the same outcome, so for the purposes of this lesson, I'll concentrate on the AIDA format.

You want to catch the reader's eye and tempt them to keep reading. What you need is a headline, just like what you'd see in an advertisement that captures your interest. You won't achieve this by offering what everyone else does, so you need to be creative and unique.

Make the reader feel that you are the perfect person for the job and must be interviewed.

Depending on the type of role you are applying for, you should begin with a statement about something you have achieved, relative to that role. For business leaders it could be about increasing the share price and profits, for finance professionals it could be a public listing, implementations of new systems, or some merger & acquisition activity. For marketing professionals, it could be one or more successful product launches.

The statement shouldn't be more than 1 or 2 lines, just like an effective headline. This is the opening remark that should attract the attention of your reader and influence them to keep reading.

I - Interest

Now that you have the reader's attention, you must reinforce it. The best way to do this is to offer facts about your achievements and quantifiable competencies (skills, knowledge and attributes) eg; an MBA qualification is a quantifiable competency, whereas 'I am a proven leader' is not.

D - Desire

Now bring your past to the present and maybe even paint a quick picture of the future - what the reader's company will be like with you in it. Relate your achievements and quantifiable competencies to the job and company at hand, to make the reader feel that you are the perfect person for the job and must be interviewed.

Now compel the reader to see you.

A - Action

Now you compel the reader to see you. Offer your phone number and email address and commit to calling them if they haven't called you in 72 hours. It is essential, once you have the reader interested in you, to make it as easy as possible to contact you.

This persuasive cover letter should never be longer than 1 page in length, as you are not writing a novel. Use bullet points to emphasise your achievements and competencies.

Summary

In summary, with proper planning, thinking and creativity, your cover letter will transform from a boring list of opinion based motherhood statements, to a fact driven, concise and influential document that will compliment your resume and get you that interview.

LESSON 04

The interview survival guide

Congratulations, the company of your dreams wants to interview you. You've impressed them enough with your resume and now comes the most important event - the meeting that could end up changing your life.

I speak with many people around the world, who openly admit attending interviews without doing any formal preparation, even though they consider the opportunity so important to their future.

As with any goal requiring exceptional performance, you have to practice the function to become excellent at the function.

I encourage you to use this 'Interview Survival Guide' as the basis of your interview training. Regardless of whether it's your 1st or 101st interview, please study the advice again and again as you will always remind yourself of at least one crucial 'do' or 'don't' and give yourself many more chances to succeed. I'll break the guide into 8 parts:

1. Preparing for the interview
2. What to do at the interview
3. What not to do at the interview
4. How to end the interview
5. What to do after the interview
6. What are some classic interview questions to be aware of?
7. The best ways to fail at interviews
8. Summary

Whether you're being interviewed or being the interviewer, please study this - it works. Okay, let's begin with:

01 Preparing for the interview

(Remember, good preparation enhances exceptional performance)

- **What is the name of the company?** How many people are you seeing and who are they (names and titles)? How many will you see at one time (one, two, is it a panel interview)? Where is the interview being held? What time is the interview? How are you going to get to the interview? How is the interview being conducted (face to face, telephone, videoconference)? How long will the interview take?

- **What do you know about the company?** Find out what you can about their global, regional and local operations. What goods & services do they provide? Where are they ranked in their market and who are their competitors? These days you can find an incredible amount of information through the Internet, but don't just look at the company's own website as it may be subjective. There are general websites that provide information on companies as well as financial websites, which are useful for publicly listed companies

What have you done that has taken you to where you are today?

- **What have you done that has taken you to where you are today? Why have you done it?** Reflect on not only your resume, but also your life achievements and disappointments, because the world's best companies like to know what their people are made of. When reviewing your resume, make sure you are able to verbalise your career history concisely and persuasively. Take a spare copy of your resume to the interview

- Not only should you **be an expert on your current company** (including it's recent share price history if a publicly listed company), but you should also have a good knowledge of each of your old companies and a brief understanding of what they are doing now

- **What are you going to ask them when it's your turn for questions?** The company is trying to ascertain if you're right for them, but you are also trying to ascertain if the company and its people are right for you. Take time to prepare a number of relevant open questions (where, why, how, what, who, when, and which) so you can discover your important information. Ask yourself the questions. Do they make sense? Would you be willing to answer them if asked? Do they make you sound impressive?
- **Practice your interview in front of the mirror or someone you can trust for an honest opinion.** Focus on your body language, posture, attitude, appearance and vocal delivery (clear and medium paced)

02 What to do at the interview

- **Always aim to be five minutes early.** Not only is it professional, but it also gives you time to relax yourself and prepare your thoughts for the meeting. Make a positive impression on the reception staff. You may need their help soon
- **Switch off your mobile phone**. Unless there is a family emergency, there is no excuse to leave it on, and even then you must forewarn the interviewer that there is a chance you will be interrupted during the meeting
- **Greet the interviewer(s) with warmth and sincerity and use his/her name**. Offer a firm and confident handshake and maintain eye contact whenever possible. Sit down only when invited and focus on your posture, without appearing to be too stiff (i.e.; you will feel more comfortable with your jacket unbuttoned). If the meeting room is hot, ask permission to remove your jacket before doing so
- It is said that the average adult forms 11 different impressions about another adult in the first 7 seconds of their first meeting. You will assess the interviewer as you are being assessed, which should help set the scene for the meeting. If there is an opportunity to break the ice, do so, as it will relax everyone and may even establish some common ground that neither of you knew existed

- **Thank the interviewer** for taking the time to meet with you and emphasise your interest in the organisation.Then confirm the agenda, as you understand it from your preparation. This shows that you are prepared and alerts you to any changes in the agenda that you need to be ready for
- **Answer questions with conviction, confidence, honesty and charisma.** Try to avoid going off on tangents unless it emphasises a point you are making. If you don't know the answer to a question, be honest. If you think a question has a negative connotation, don't be afraid to provide negative examples. These questions are designed to see how you overcome adversity and what lessons you learn in the process. Trying to be too positive when faced with such a question may make an interviewer wonder what you're trying to hide. The world's best companies need people who can strive through both the good and bad times

- When you ask questions, **prove that you are an even better listener than talker.** Paraphrase if necessary to clarify important points from answers given to you
- **Try to get the interviewer to describe the opportunity early on in the meeting** so you can tailor the major highlights of your background to the role and emphasise your relevant competencies
- **Ask the interviewer to repeat a question if you miss it the first time**. Some candidates feel embarrassed and try to guess what was said - this is unnecessary
- **Be yourself.** This is not the time to be putting on an act in order to impress and/or conform, as the real you may end up working with this company

Okay, now let's talk about:

03 What NOT to do at the interview

- **Avoid making negative comments** about your current or previous employers, bosses, peers or subordinates, unless directly asked for by the interviewer (you may be asked "What was the worst thing about ....?"). Just don't overdo it
- **Avoid even the slightest discriminatory remarks**. You may have said it in jest, but it may have just cost you the job
- **Avoid asking about remuneration at the first meeting**. If the interviewer brings the subject up, then discuss it, but don't dwell on it
- **Avoid telling the interviewer you're not interested in the opportunity and/or the company** even if you're not. Twenty four hours of reflection can result in a more accurate and rational decision

The next thing for you to consider is:

04 How to end the interview

- If you are interested in the opportunity and the company, then tell the interviewer in a confident and enthusiastic manner. **Ask what the next step of the process will be and establish an indicative timetable**. Commit to the next step immediately if the opportunity presents itself
- If the interviewer offers you the position at the first interview, **ask for some time** (at least twenty-four hours) to think about it, regardless of how interested you are. You need to make a rational decision
- The interviewer may ask you if you are considering other opportunities. **If you are, be honest**, as not only does it show that you are the 'hottest product in the market', but it also helps the company with their own timetable and agenda so that decisions can be made on time for both parties
- **Feel free to ask how many people the interviewer is interviewing,** if it helps manage your expectations of the process. You shouldn't appear any less confident whether the company is interviewing 100 people or just you
- Although you may feel that the interview hasn't gone well, **don't despair**, as the interviewer could have every intention of pursuing you, but may appear non-committal just to solicit a reaction from you
- Close the meeting by **thanking the interviewer for the time committed** and leave a positive lasting impression on them as you say goodbye

Thank the reception staff on your way out.

- And don't forget to thank the reception staff on your way out - they are an important ally.

Now for:

05 What to do after the interview

(the "do I" or "don't I" stage)

- If you've been presented for the interview by a recruitment company, then as soon as time permits, call the consultant who presented you for the opportunity and talk through the experience. How did you feel in the interview? How do you think the interviewer(s) felt? How do you feel now? How do you think the company feels about you? Where do you go from here?
- You will need some time to reflect on the meeting and start moving towards a rational decision about your intentions. You should make a list of the pros and cons of the job and the company, maybe even the industry if it's a new one for you. What is the list telling you? You may even think of a number of points, which require further clarification to help you with your decision. Make sure you get answers to them. Discuss your scenario with 2 or 3 people who you trust and listen to their opinions
- Be honest with those people about how you're feeling, as any doubt you may have could have been caused by a simple misinterpretation of information, which can be easily addressed and result in a more informed decision being made

06 What are some classic interview questions to be aware of?

- Why are you interested in this opportunity and our company?
- What difference will you make to our organisation?
- Why do you want to leave your current position and what are you looking for?
- What are your weaknesses and how are you overcoming them?

What would you do differently if you had your time over again?

- What lesson have you learned from each position you have had?
- What would you do differently if you had your time over again?
- What management style gets the best out of you? How would your staff describe you as a manager?
- What are the two biggest risks you have taken in the last three years?
- Why will you accept our offer if we make you one?

Now I want to talk about:

07 The best ways to fail at the interview

(and how you should avoid these at all costs)

- Weak handshake and/or not standing up to shake hands
- Lack of eye contact
- Lack of interest, charisma and passion
- Noticeably late without a good reason or apology
- Making too many negative remarks about current or past employers, bosses, peers and subordinates

- Lack of preparation for interview. Little or no knowledge of the interviewer's company, resulting in weak, if any questions being asked by the candidate
- Lack of confidence and conviction
- Lack of logical continuity in candidate's background and poor reasons provided
- Making remuneration appear more important than the opportunity and company
- Behaving like a 'know it all' - being over confident and arrogant
- Poor listener
- Poorly presented
- Leave mobile phone on in interview and accept calls
- Poor communication skills - incorrect grammar and lacking clarity of speech
- Not willing to share negative experiences and mistakes for fear of looking inferior
- Weak body language
- Lack of initiative
- Lack of manners/common courtesy/tact

08 In summary

Remember to use this 'Interview Survival Guide' as your MUST DO checklist for every interview that you ever attend. The only reason you should ever stop using it is when you can recite it word for word. Make a mental tick against each idea every time you use the guide, to guarantee that you have all of your bases covered and ensure that your interview is that much closer to being a complete success. You can even add to the guide as you continue to learn from each interview experience, whether you're being interviewed or if, in fact, you're the interviewer.

LESSON 05

How to be a better public speaker

Speaking in public - just the thought of it makes many people freeze with terror, sweat profusely, and go mentally blank. It is believed through many surveys, that most people fear public speaking more than they fear death.

To be honest, I don't know what percentage of those surveyed were in the active workforce, however, many workforce participants would avoid speaking in public too often if they could help it.

Once you are working at a senior level in an organisation, it is inevitable that you will be presenting to a group, whether internally or externally.

You may be training internal staff, speaking at an industry seminar, pitching for business, or addressing shareholders at an annual general meeting, but in all cases, you will be in the spotlight, performing solo, and viewed by your audience as the expert in the field of your speech. There are some invaluable golden rules to follow for the preparation and delivery of your presentation.

Let's start with:

The topic of your presentation - what is it?

It is imperative that you know the exact wording of the topic that you have been asked to speak on, so that there is no confusion between what you say and what your audience is expecting you to say. You need to decide on a definition of each word of the topic and structure your content around those definitions eg; the topic may contain the phrase 'short term', so you need to decide what time period 'short term' is, so that your audience tunes into your wavelength straight away.

Who is the audience?

How many people will be attending your presentation? What are their backgrounds? Are they experts in the field of your topic, do they know anything about your topic, are they academics, commercial executives,

students? Do you know roughly how old they are, the predominant gender, are they paying to attend or is it free? Are they strangers to you or do you know them? Is English their first or second language?

The more accurate the information you have about your audience, the better you can structure your content and delivery style.

Things you need to know on the day

How many speakers are there? How long are they speaking for compared with you? How long are you speaking for? What number speaker are you? Will someone introduce you, or are you introducing yourself? Does the venue have all necessary AV equipment that you'll need? Can you test the equipment in advance? Will you stand at a lectern or be sitting down, and where will you rest your notes?

Deliver a smaller number of well made points.

What are you going to say?

Will your speech be based on fact or opinion or both? Will the opinion be yours or someone else's that you've found in your research? Will you simply repackage information that you have heard or read elsewhere, or will you reflect on your own personal experience and offer anecdotes? What will the mix be between theoretical and practical information?

When preparing your content, be mindful of overdoing the volume of information. Delivering a smaller number of well made points will be much better received and respected than many poorly made points.

You are better off being specific, original, insightful, concise and fresh, rather than trying to deliver too much information, which could cause you to rush, trivialise, and lose connectivity with your audience.

Prepare notes in point form that you can quickly refer to, without having to take your eyes off your audience for very long. You can't afford to lose that connection, so you should rehearse what you will say until you are confident you can maintain maximum eye contact. If you are using PowerPoint or other audio-visual display, you should avoid looking at the screen behind you and concentrate on the people in front of you.

Now let's talk about:

Structuring and delivering your presentation,

which comprises 4 sections:

1. Introduction
Your beginning needs to have energy, instantly engaging your audience and tuning them into your wavelength. Outline what you're going to talk about in a way that makes the audience see your content as innovative, provoking, and important.

Don't use humour unless you are funny and totally confident that your joke will appeal to and not offend your audience. Attempted humour that falls flat, will only embarrass you and make your audience feel uneasy.

2. The main body of your presentation
Think about each of the points you have decided to talk about. How would you rank them in terms of importance to one another? These rankings will help you allocate the appropriate amount of time to each

point and impress upon the audience what is most important about what you're saying. Be aware of any tangents that you may go off on, as they can cause your speech to lose its balance and tempo.

Your content should continue to flow in a way that takes your audience from one point to the next with ease. You are the driver and you want your passengers moving with you at the same pace.

Your ending is as important as your beginning.

If you decide to quote other people, make sure you get their name right and what it is that makes them qualified to be included in your speech.

3. Conclusion

Your ending is as important as your beginning. You want to leave your audience on a high, wanting you to keep talking. Take the audience back to your central point and reinforce your main argument, as it will help them remember what you've said. Avoid introducing new ideas that you may have forgotten to include earlier. Allow your conclusion to flow logically and leave your listeners satisfied.

4. Timing

Being nervous, allowing questions mid-speech, trying to include an idea you just thought of, problems with your audio-visual equipment. How many of us have suffered at least one of these dilemmas when speaking in public? Your timing can go right off and you may then struggle to regain the smooth logical flow you started with.

Should you feel that you won't finish on time due to these unforseen delays, then focus on your conclusion and make sure you get that right, as per your rehearsal, as this is what you will leave your audience with to remember you by. Make it powerful.

What about:

Taking questions from the audience?

If you have allowed time for audience questions, then you have the perfect opportunity to consolidate the perception that you are an expert in your field. There are a few important things to be aware of when taking questions:

- Repeat questions back before answering to ensure that the whole audience hears it

- Don't offer an answer if you don't have a knowledgeable one. You are not expected to know everything so don't pretend to.
- Respect the question asker with eye contact when answering.
- Make sure you fully understand the wording and context of the question before attempting to answer

Let's finish with:

Practicing your presentation

You have worked hard gathering information for your presentation and structuring it so that you will deliver a first class speech within the allocated time - in theory anyway. The final step of the process is to actually practice your presentation. Using a video camera can help, but better still is to have a few trusted friends and/or colleagues act as your audience. You can trust them to tell you the truth about your style and content.

They will give you feedback on the non-verbal communication elements of your presentation style: the way you stand, eye contact, facial expressions, gestures, talking speed, whether you are relaxed or tense, your level of intimacy and impact, the melody of your voice. You should also experiment with your timing, making sure that your allocation makes sense.

You are not expected to know everything so don't pretend to.

Best of luck with your next presentation. Preparation and practice (better in front of a friend than the mirror) will increase the probability of a successful speech, a happy speaker and a happy audience.

I'm happy to recommend that you consider joining your local Toastmasters speaking club if you are serious about improving your public speaking ability. These clubs are supportive, encouraging and constructive, and its members are there for the same reason. For more information about Toastmasters, see www.toastmasters.org. I've known many people over the years who have praised Toastmasters for helping them not only overcome their fears of public speaking, but also become accomplished presenters.

LESSON 06

How do you handle counter offers?

Congratulations, you've just accepted an offer for the job you've been chasing for months. You are excited and relieved, but you're wondering how your boss is going to react when you resign. Will your boss be understanding, angry, shocked or dismissive? How do you react when one of your best performers resigns to you?

Some of the more common thoughts that the boss may have are:

- Damn it, she's one of my best performers. How am I supposed to replace her, keep the team together, and achieve budget?
- What inconvenient timing – I was about to go on annual vacation for 2 weeks
- How am I going to look to senior management for losing this person?
- Where is she going?
- Can I get her to stay until I find a replacement and have an effective hand over?
- How can I get her to stay?

If you are a valuable resource, then your boss and your company won't want to see you walk out the door, especially to the competition. They will make every attempt to convince you to stay, either by:

You have only received a counter offer because you resigned.

- Making you a counter offer
- Making you feel incredibly guilty and disloyal
- 'Loving' you like they've never 'loved' you before – be suspicious of this approach

Being made an attractive counter offer is instantly good for your ego, but you must take a number of things into consideration before saying "thanks" or "no thanks":

- You have only received a counter offer because you resigned. It is a purely reactive tactic from your employer and should make you wonder whether you need to resign every time you want to improve your situation. If your employer thought you were truly worthy, why didn't they improve your situation anyway?
- Do your reasons for wanting to leave still exist? You may have a number of reasons – salary too low, no promotion in sight, don't like your boss. You may be offered more money to stay, which can be tempting, but if you still have other issues outstanding, you'll probably end up leaving anyway

- Despite what your employer is saying to you, they will probably now consider you a risk and may make contingency plans without your knowledge. You may not be seen as a true member of the team
- The counter offer could simply be an interim tactic from your employer to bridge a gap whilst they look to replace you

Much research and many surveys have been completed over the years to measure what happens to employees who accept counter offers. Only a small percentage are still with their company after 12 months, and 2 important points become apparent:

- Salary was hardly ever the prime motivator for resigning – more money didn't ultimately change the true state of play
- Things didn't take long to return to the way they were before the resignation

Before accepting a counter offer, ask yourself why your employer has made the offer. There is a strong possibility that the cons will outweigh the pros and you will realise that your decision to resign was right after all.

LESSON 07

Time – you only get one chance to use it

How well do you manage your time? You know that you only have 168 hours each week to fit your entire life into, made up of the things that you want to do and the things that you need to do.

Work, rest and play are the 3 major events in your life and it is how you manage your time across each of these events that can determine how successful you actually become.

Let's face it, there are great time managers and there are not so great time managers. The great time managers simply get more done than everybody else and most likely feel a much greater sense of accomplishment. They have a good knowledge of how they use their time and have quite often developed effective habits to know what to do and when to do it – in other words, they know how to prioritise.

Let's look at establishing priorities

I'd like you to pick up a pen and draw the following diagram, which is designed to help you prioritise all of the things that you try to get done each day. On a sheet of paper, I want you to write on the left side of the page, about a third of the way down, the word 'Urgent'. Now go down another third and write the words 'Not Urgent'. Across the top of the page, I want you to write the word 'Important' about a third across the page, and then another third across, write the words 'Not Important'. Now that you have that done, next step is to write the letter A where Urgent and Important intersect, the letter B where Urgent and Not Important intersect, the letter C where Not Urgent and Important intersect and finally, the letter D where Not Urgent and Not Important intersect.

You can use this diagram to rate each of your daily tasks and prioritise effectively. You'll be amazed at how many of the things that you really want to do, actually get done.

	Important	**Not Important**
Urgent	A	B
Not Urgent	C	D

When you review the tasks you have included in the Not Important/ Not Urgent section, ask yourself whether you need to do these tasks at all. These tasks can generally be either delegated or dismissed completely.

Now, let's look at some classic time management pitfalls:

- Email – reading, responding, composing
- Written work eg; reports, proposals – both composing and reading
- Long telephone calls
- Not taking the call now – asking for a message to be taken
- Meetings and timing of meetings
- Lack of planning
- Lack of effective delegation
- Not knowing the difference between what is urgent and what is important

Here are some time management tips:

Email

- Block out times in your diary to use email – 15 minutes in the morning, lunchtime and late afternoon. You know how much of your day can be consumed by email activity if you're not disciplined, so you need to take control of it

Written work

- Dictate as much as possible, then have it typed by your personal assistant (PA) or other administrative assistant
- Your PA should be able to produce a standard proposal for you, which you can then fine tune

Telephone calls

- You control the conversation
- Take the call now, not a message
- If phone messages are being taken for you, make sure the message taker alerts your PA, who should know what needs to be addressed now, versus later

If your role involves visiting clients

- Try to do them on your way to work and on your way home
- Organise visits based on geography where possible i.e., see 2 or 3 clients in a row if they are based in the same building

Don't procrastinate ... if it is important, do it now.

- Make sure the person is worth seeing – have you qualified them properly, especially if they are a long way from your office?
- Invite the client to your offices
- Don't wait more than 20 minutes if the client is running late – reschedule

Planning

- Use a 'to do' list – a well maintained to do list is one of the simplest and most effective means of organising your day. You should complete it either just before you go home at night or first thing in the morning before you start work
- Start with priority tasks – rate each of your tasks with an A, B or C rating with A being highest priority. Once you have finished rating your list, work through the As first, then B to C and maintain your focus on completing the list
- Don't procrastinate – If it is important, do it now

- Break up large tasks into smaller easily managed units – What can seem daunting or even impossible as a whole, can become manageable when broken into components. Allocate expected time to completion for each component
- Learn to say no when you need to – Saying no when you don't want interruptions can be a valuable way of keeping control of your own time frame. If you find this difficult, then you may need some assertion training
- Find a quiet space – You will achieve much more when you can devote chunks of time to a task without interruption. Find a spare office or meeting room, divert your phone (mobile & fixed line), and lock yourself away for an agreed time
- Do similar tasks at the one time – If you have a number of minor but related tasks to do, eg; returning telephone calls, wait until you have a decent number of them and then return them all in one session. You will save yourself interruptions and may even manage each call more efficiently
- Avoid over commitment – Be realistic about what you can do in any given time and always allow time for the inevitable crises. They can't be avoided but their effect can be minimised

Meetings

- Be on time, start on time, finish on time and respect other people's time
- Keep meetings out of core hours
- Make sure the meeting is needed in the first place
- I once read about a company that holds its meetings standing up, so that nobody gets too comfortable and time isn't wasted

Effective delegation to your PA

- Establish a team approach on a professional basis
- Develop a good working relationship based on mutual respect

- Involve your PA in the entire process of what you are doing, so that your PA is in a good position to properly service your external and internal customers:

    - Have a quick daily meeting each morning to update on the day's priorities. Inform your PA of any projects, and provide a brief overview of the key contacts involved (external and/or internal)

    - Encourage those contacts to liaise with your PA when you are unavailable

    - Communicate deadlines to your PA in advance

    - Ensure that your PA understands why a task is a priority; this should make their job more interesting and result in happy customers

    - Forward plan as much as possible and at all times attempt to maximise productivity. Stick to your deadlines.

    - If you are busy, don't forget that your PA will be too, therefore:

    - Don't leave things to the last minute

    - Don't request urgent work, and then leave it lying around for a day. You should avoid this if you have properly rated the priority of your tasks

    - Don't take your stress out on your PA

    - Bring urgent work to your PA's attention – don't just leave it in your out tray

    - Don't make unrealistic promises with impossible deadlines to your clients (to your PA, there is a huge difference between 5pm today and 9am tomorrow)

- Return your telephone calls promptly to avoid callers continually calling back. If you know you are going to be unavailable, ask your PA to pass on any necessary information that you are being contacted for

These time management tips will help free up a few more hours in your diary each week. People tell me how much better they feel knowing that they have more control over their schedule, as well as feeling more effective, efficient and empowered.

LESSON 08

How to induct a new employee

Now, the new employee being inducted could be you, or you could be inducting someone you've just hired. Either way, starting a new role should be an exciting event, but it can also be a very stressful experience for an individual, regardless of their level in the organisation.

They need to meet many new people, absorb many new systems, procedures and ideologies, and quickly understand the performance expectations that the company and their immediate boss have of them.

Through efficient and effective induction, you are providing your new employee with the necessary information and resources to become comfortable and productive as quickly as possible. The sooner you can align them with the culture, goals, and expectations of your organisation, your team, and how the various staff, teams, and divisions relate to one another, the sooner the new employee will be effective as an individual and as a team member.

There are 3 main objectives when inducting a new employee:

1. To align them with the organisation
2. To align them with their immediate team
3. To help them understand their role, so that they can be productive sooner

When carried out in this order, each achieved objective makes the next objective easier to understand and achieve.

By promptly aligning your new employee with the organisation and the team, you provide them with the greatest opportunity to 'tune in' to the wavelength of the company and its people and be able to make a greater contribution sooner, as an integral member of their new family.

Let's look at the path to induction

These days there are organisations that place so much importance on effective induction, that they formalise their induction process so to include it as part of their QA procedures under ISO standards. Such a process ensures that all new employees have the opportunity to integrate into the company from a consistent platform.

It is imperative that the new employee's induction has the full support of their manager and that the manager has an active involvement in the 3 stage process. A typical process may comprise the following events and although a number of them may look very basic, they all send important messages to the new member of the team.

Okay, so what are the objectives?

Objective 1 – Alignment with the organisation

- The manager welcomes the new employee on their arrival, takes them to their desk, introduces them to their immediate team, and then leaves them to get familiar with their immediate surroundings. This can also be a good time for them to talk with their personal assistant (if applicable) about housekeeping issues, desk management, etc
- The manager takes the employee for a meet and greet session through the office, as well as making the employee aware of office facilities. The employee's comfort level continues to increase during this process
- They then finish the tour by reacquainting the employee with their allocated 'buddy'
- A meeting is organised with finance and human resources departments to go through administrative formalities eg; tax, payroll and pension benefit forms. Salary packaging options, if any, can also be discussed
- Company information is provided to the new employee for personal reading and digestion eg; company brochure, internet and intranet orientation, internal telephone and email directories
- A session is organised by the manager, where a presentation is made to the new employee by either their manager or a more senior executive, on company philosophy, direction,

vision and mission, ethics and some overview of internal company mechanics

- The manager or 'buddy' organises lunch with the new employee on the first day. All 3 should attend
- The new employee also needs some 'self time' to be able to absorb the heavy load of information that has been provided
- The manager then checks in with the new employee at the end of the first day to make sure everything ran smoothly and to answer initial questions that the new employee may have. The 'buddy' should also make sure that the new employee has got through the first day okay

Let me explain the 'buddy' system

A 'buddy' is any member of your organisation who you, the manager, consider to be a person who reflects the company's values and possesses the core competencies (skills, knowledge & attributes) that the new employee will ultimately need, to be a successful contributor.

The 'buddy' is quite often one of the senior management team who was involved in the interview process and has a sense of influence. Try to avoid appointing a member of your own team as the 'buddy', as it's best to offer a more objective person to this task who is at least one step removed from your team.

Objective 2 – Alignment with the team

- The manager provides the new employee with a history, current overview, and proposed future of their immediate department. The manager also explains how the department interacts with other departments eg; sales with finance, marketing with IT, human resources with human resources in other offices
- The manager should organise lunch with the new employee and other immediate team members, to share experiences in a less formal setting and help continue to increase the comfort and confidence of the new employee
- The manager should continue to have catch-up sessions with the new employee, to ensure that all is okay and be able to avoid any misunderstandings or misconceptions

Objective 3 – to help them understand their role, so that they can be productive sooner

- The manager organises designated times with different senior staff and managers throughout the company, for them to inform and train the new employee in specific job functions eg; taking a brief from a client (sales), structuring internal training (HR), using the company intranet (IT), following up with slow paying clients (finance), liaising with media, shareholders and analysts re company results (investor relations)
- These sessions can be many and varied, but in totality will provide the new employee with the necessary breadth of job

competencies. You can decide what to include, depending on your industry and department focus

- The sessions will also depend on the new employee's prior experience and ability. Each session should be no longer than 1 hour, at which time extra information can be provided for the new employee's own private study
- Some of these internal sessions may be complimented with 'out in the field' sessions, visiting clients etc. I have seen many business developers take a member of the finance team to meet a new client, so to consolidate the relationship and make the ground rules clear for future dealings

How long should the induction take?

It is recommended that the induction process take between 1 and 2 months, with the majority completed in the first 5-6 weeks. Any sessions can and should be repeated if deemed necessary by either party, because the most effective induction process requires that both the new employee and the manager sign off on the satisfactory completion of each component of the induction.

The job competency sessions should be reasonably spaced, to ensure that the new employee doesn't suffer from information overload and thus negatively affecting absorption rates and perhaps even requiring sessions to be repeated unnecessarily. These sessions will also help identify gaps in the new employee's competencies, for which an ongoing training and development program can be prepared.

By breaking down the induction into a logical sequence of 'bite size' sessions, the new employee can not only better manage their own timetable, but they will complete the process, achieve sign off from their manager, and be in the best possible position. They will be aligned with the organisation, aligned with the team, and understand their role so that they can start making a successful contribution to themselves and their new company.

Induction will help identify gaps in the new employee's competencies.

Whether you're starting a new job or hiring someone to work for you, use this induction process and I'm sure that all parties will enjoy the transition a lot more and appreciate the extra effort, leading to greater loyalty right from the start.

LESSON 09

A quick guide to giving and receiving feedback

Feedback – most of us can't get enough of it when it's positive, and would rather avoid it when it's negative. In every organisation, you will at some time either be giving feedback or receiving it, whether you are praising a staff member, disciplining your assistant, or going through your own performance review with your boss.

Feedback, both positive and negative, can have a dramatic impact on the person receiving it, and in many cases, the feedback is given on a spur of the moment basis with the primary intent being more emotional than rational. I believe there are a number of simple rules that you should keep in mind for the feedback that you are giving or receiving to be used to its greatest effect.

Try to remain rational rather than emotional.

Receiving feedback

Let's start with receiving feedback.
There are 6 points I'd like to make here:

1. Your aim should be to **seek feedback** rather than always waiting for it to come to you or not expecting any at all. I have seen cases where performance reviews are postponed due to busy schedules, then forgotten about completely. That loss of a structured forum for feedback can be detrimental to your ongoing development and success, because you are left guessing about how you're really progressing

2. **Accept praise graciously** and take criticism as constructive advice. Try to remain rational rather than emotional, sensitive and defensive. Also correct any inaccurate information factually and confidently

3. **Listen well, concentrate and take notes if necessary for further follow up**. Ask for time if you feel you need to digest the information before responding

4. **Restate the feedback** in order to guarantee your understanding of what has been said to you. Ask for more information if necessary as well as specific suggestions about how you could improve

5. Whether the feedback is positive or negative, **look for agreement from your reviewer on, 'Where to from here?' to ensure that the feedback doesn't go to waste**

6. **Follow up, follow up, follow up**

Giving feedback

Now, here are 6 key points about giving feedback to someone else:

1. **Look at the person and speak directly to them**. Be confident and credible

2. **Be timely –** if you have organised a meeting for you to give feedback, then make sure that you follow through on that commitment. In the case of spur of the moment feedback, try to act as closely as possible to the time that the particular behaviour occurred and in time for any agreed changes to be made

3. **Be specific** – provide factual examples and offer constructive advice on how the behaviour might be changed to improve future outcomes

4. **Praise the person where possible**

5. **Be aware of how the person is reacting to your feedback.** Adjust your style if necessary and show both courtesy and discretion

6. **Avoid getting too personal** – you can let the person know how their behaviour made you feel, but don't overdo it

This is a brief but relevant guide to feedback. Unique circumstances will require a unique approach at times, but the ideas listed above can be used in all situations and increase the probability of an effective and successful discussion.

LESSON 10

Successful one minute, mediocre the next

Humans want to be successful. We all have different definitions of the word 'success' but whatever our definition is, we all aim to achieve that definition. You may want to be successful at work, love, sport, as a leader, as a follower. Whilst being successful is a wonderful feeling, many of us don't exactly know how to manage this success, nor how to maintain it.

We set goals and we strive to achieve them. Once these are achieved, we can suddenly become complacent and switch our motors to autopilot. There don't appear to be any higher goals to set and suddenly we find the competition invading our turf.

In any competitive arena, this sudden sense of falling behind can reignite the spark to succeed again. This relates to the widest variety of cases, from suddenly falling behind in a tennis match, to realising that you've been neglecting your spouse, to seeing your sales figures plummet.

We all deserve some time off to reflect on the satisfaction of achieving goals, and feeling successful, but if that time off drags on for too long, then you face the risk of falling behind and suffering mediocrity. You will always be answerable to the standards that you set for yourself, so if you have sought success and achieved it, then the taste seldom leaves you, and anything less is not an easy thing to live with.

When you look at popular business lists such as Fortune 500, you see that over the years, businesses come and go, even the largest ones. These companies and no doubt many of their senior management, fail to move with the times and reset goals for the future. Whilst they are being complacent, their smaller, hungrier and more goal oriented competitors overtake them.

Most human beings should be called human doings, because we are always doing things. It is important to take some time to simply 'be' and switch off for a while. Some people turn to meditation, yoga, listening to music or just sitting on the beach. When we feel successful, we deserve to celebrate, but we also need to reaffirm our vision and make sure that we are still on the right road to where we want to be.

LESSON 11

How do you look for a new job?

At some stage in your career, you will almost certainly be looking for a new job. This may be because you're not truly satisfied in your current job, or simply because you're unemployed. I haven't met many people who say that they enjoy the job search process, which is unfortunate, as the search for a new job should be all about renewal, progress and self-growth.

There are job searchers who take a long time to secure a new job and those who manage to find a new job quite quickly and without too much effort or stress. If you look at the typical character traits of successful job seekers, there tends to be a common theme amongst the way they handle themselves and their search.

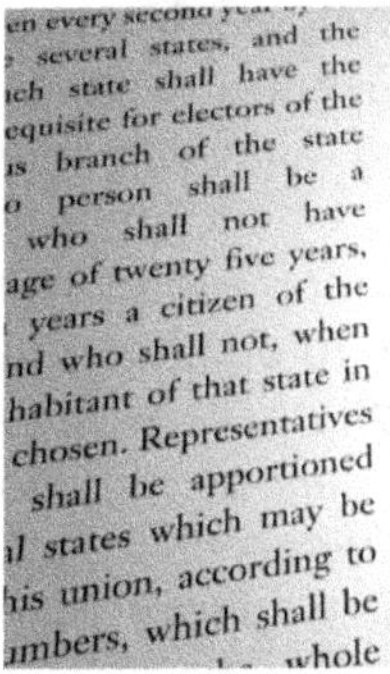

Here are 6 common traits:

1. **Self-awareness** – which is the ability to assess your strengths and weaknesses with honesty and objectivity. You understand the impact you have on other people and tailor your approach accordingly to each situation. You are also willing to experience the emotional reactions towards you for being without a job, should you ever be in such a situation

2. **Receptivity** – your willingness to accept support from others, and being open to learning and change

3. **Commercial acumen** – the ability to take a business oriented approach, viewing yourself as a product, understanding the potential employer's business objectives, and marketing yourself appropriately

4. **Focus** – the ability to focus on clearly defined goals, being proactive, committed to success, and well organized

5. **Positive attitude** – the ability to maintain your self-belief and strive to achieve the desired result

6. **Resourcefulness** – the ability to identify and leverage necessary information, people, and other resources to achieve success

Ask yourself, and perhaps those close to you, how many of those traits you possess and what you might need to develop them further. You may even be able to help someone else develop the traits.

> **Asking for a referral takes a certain level of self-confidence and courage.**

It continues to amaze me how narrowly some people structure their job search. There are those who answer job ads that they see in the newspaper or on internet job sites, then there are those who send their CV to employment agencies and wait to receive a call offering them their perfect job opportunity. Obviously these are vital components of a successful job search strategy, however they are not the way that most people find a new job.

So, what are some of the other key components of a successful job search strategy?

Networking with friends/family/ex-colleagues

Most job seekers find their new job this way. Employers like nothing better than to hire new staff that their own employees have recommended. This is such an important job search method, but many job seekers don't employ it as they are reluctant to ask the

people closest to them for help. Asking for a referral takes a certain level of self-confidence and courage, and many people have a natural reluctance to make such a request.

Let me share a brief story with you to illustrate this approach. In early 1998, when my beautiful wife, Jacinda, and I were living and working in Hong Kong, she was at a café, enjoying lunch with a friend. She told her friend that she was interested in finding a new job and asked her friend to keep an eye out for her, as she was well connected in the Hong Kong market. Within 3 days, Jacinda received a phone call from her wonderful friend. She had heard about an opportunity and passed on the contact details of the decision maker at the company. Jacinda called the company and was told that she had come highly recommended by her friend. Two interviews later and she had the job – a job she enjoyed for 3 years and then left with great references and life long friends.

Networking at industry events

Let me share a true story with you which serves as a classic example of being rewarded for having the courage and self-belief to network at an industry event.

Back in 1998, when I was living in Hong Kong as an executive recruiter, I interviewed a Korean born Australian (let's call him Scott), who had just arrived in Hong Kong, in search of a new career adventure. Scott had excellent qualifications and experience, but above all else, he came across as a very capable, likeable and positive individual. I told him straight out that I thought he was an excellent prospect and that I'd help all I could, however, he was going to find his job search challenging through the employment agency and job classified channels, as he didn't have any local Hong Kong work experience, which seemed to be of vital importance to most companies.

I told Scott that his best chance of success was to take a broad approach to his job search and start networking as soon as possible. I invited him to a Chamber of Commerce function the following evening that I was attending, where I could introduce him to the people I knew. Scott attended the function, and in advance had some business cards printed, with his name, phone number, and email address on the front, and a brief statement about what he was looking for on the back of the card, along with a few personal USPs to entice the reader. I introduced him around and then watched, as he met many other attendees, swapping business cards with them and sharing positive energy.

One attendee, the Asia Pacific President of a major telecommunications company, really hit it off with Scott, and invited him for a formal interview the following morning, to discuss a potential role in regional business development. I actually knew about that job, as I was pitching for the chance to recruit it the following day. I arrived the following day at 12 o'clock, just as the President and Scott came out of his office, smiling I might add. "Sorry," the President said to me as we shook hands, "looks like you're too late!" He felt he had found the perfect person and there was no need to look any further. Scott joined the company, and exceeded expectations to such an extent, that he was promoted within 2 years to run the company's fast growing Korean operations.

His best chance of success was to take a broad approach.

There are various industry events you should consider attending, meeting other attendees, giving them your business card, and making a positive impression on them. These events include:

- Chamber of Commerce
- Industry seminars
- Professional associations eg; CPA
- Job fairs

Direct approach to potential employers

Many job seekers seem to think that the only way they can gain direct access to employers is either by applying to a job advertisement or applying through an employment agency. That couldn't be further from the truth. Once you have done some homework and accumulated a list of companies you'd be interested in working for, you should then make every effort to find out who the appropriate contact is at each company, and send them your CV directly. You can also connect with them on LinkedIn if they have a profile on the site.

From my experience, you can benefit further by trying to reach the contact first on the phone. If you make contact, then you can sell yourself a little, and then follow up with your CV. Better still, you may even manage to secure an interview over the phone and you can then simply take your CV with you to the meeting. Even if the meeting is simply an information sharing session, it is the perfect opportunity for you to 'sow the seed that you've planted' so that you'll be considered when the next opportunity arises.

> **On many of these sites, you can build a profile of the kind of job you're looking for.**

To be honest, I have found that job seekers have had most luck with this direct approach, when they have contacted functional line managers, rather than the Human Resources department. Just say you're interested in sales opportunities – you may receive more immediate interest from the Sales Director than you would from the Human Resources department, as the Sales Director will be thinking more strategically about hiring needs for the sales team and could even create a role for you if you fit the profile. If that's the case, then

you have just secured a role that will never need to be advertised in the paper, posted on a job board, or given to an employment agency – the direct and proactive approach is worth the effort.

Job classifieds (both print and online)

This is the most obvious approach undertaken by active job seekers. Applying to job advertisements in newspapers is popular, but in this technology age, this approach should be complimented by searching through online job ads, social media, etc. There are professional online networks such as LinkedIn and online job websites, such as monster.com, which frequently post new jobs that may be relevant to you. On many of these sites, you can build a profile of the kind of job you're looking for, and as long as you provide your email address, these sites will send you relevant job ads as they appear on the site. The other great benefit of these sites is that they tend to keep the jobs on their sites until they are filled, so you can apply to jobs that may have been posted to the site 2 days, 2 weeks, or even 2 months ago. You don't have this luxury with job ads in the newspaper.

Recruitment Firms

A lot of job seekers register their CV with at least one recruitment firm. This most often takes the form of an application to an advertised job, however there is no reason for you not to proactively register your CV with a number of reputable recruitment firms on a general basis, asking the recruiter to keep you on their radar for potential opportunities as they arise.

Let's look at some of the benefits of partnering with a recruitment firm to support your job search:

Third-party representation

Many job seekers prefer to have someone do their negotiating for them, when dealing with a potential employer. Just like in the real estate industry, the agent can represent the interests of both parties and ensure that the process of hiring a candidate ends in success for all concerned.

Industry Connections

Recruiters are paid on the basis of filling jobs with candidates, so you would expect that they'd be in constant contact with the market in which they operate. You can gain much faster and direct access to the employers you're interested in joining, as well as having the recruiter promote you as a preferred candidate. Having this testimonial will get you a lot more attention than if you applied directly to the employer.

Broader Market Exposure

You may have a list of companies that you're interested in working for, but a recruiter can offer ideas on an even greater selection of companies for you to consider. Good recruiters know their market, and can open you up to a wider range of options than you could have generated on your own.

Expert Training And Preparation

When a recruiter takes an interest in you, they will want to help you to be your best. To support your chances of finding a job, they may provide advice on how to improve your CV, your interview technique, networking skills, etc. This advice is nearly always free, as the recruiter is ultimately compensated for filling the job.

They do the work for you

If you're busy in your current job, it is difficult to focus on an active job search. Researching companies, looking at job advertisements, approaching potential employers – these activities take time and focus, so it can be of great benefit to let a trusted recruiter to do it for you. They handle the process and keep you updated with progress.

Okay, so what are some of the disadvantages of using a recruitment firm?

Confidentiality

Whilst this isn't a common problem in the recruitment industry, there are certain consultants who may list a new job to fill, and after finding a number of potential candidates on their database, they then forward those candidates to the employer, without gaining the candidate's permission first. This puts the candidate at considerable risk, especially if it's a company they do not wish to be disclosed to. There are other recruiters who may actually call you to get permission to send your CV to the employer, but they won't tell you who the employer is – it's up to you on this one, but personally, I would never allow my CV to be sent to a company unless I knew who that company was and was happy with it. Once your confidentiality is compromised, you could be in a vulnerable position.

Don't ever underestimate the power of showing your face and saying hello.

Losing control of the process

Let's assume that you've empowered a recruiter to represent you to a number of potential employers. These companies are 'A list' in your opinion, and you hope that the recruiter has more chance of securing you an interview than if you approached the companies directly. The process is then out of your hands and you are relying on the recruiter's ability to make it happen. Do you know what relationship the recruiter has with those companies? What if the companies prefer not to pay recruitment fees and instead recruit candidates who apply to them directly? What if the recruiter fails to secure you an interview? Do you know how hard the recruiter tried? Is it now too late for you to apply directly to the companies? You need to be convinced that by handing control of this important process to the recruiter, you will achieve the desired result.

Summary

In summary, the success rate of your job search increases greatly when you utilise the 5 methods described in this lesson. In regards to networking, don't ever underestimate the power of showing your face and saying hello. The person you've just met may not have the job opportunity you're looking for, but you should always be conscious of the '6 degrees of separation' principle.

Everybody knows someone, who knows someone else, who knows someone else, and so on. If you follow this principle and always make a positive impression on the next person you're referred to, you may well end up meeting the person who has the opportunity that you're looking for.

The key to an effective job search is to keep your ear to the ground and maintain momentum. Stay in the traffic, but take the time to step back on to the kerb once in a while to reassess your direction. Your challenge is to avoid the traffic congestion and find the less travelled route to your destination. Have you ever left home an hour early to drive to work and been rewarded with a smoother, faster, and easier journey? – I rest my case.

LESSON 12

How do you choose the right career?

You can start by designing your next job.

How many people have you met over the years who tell you that they're not sure if they're in the right career? They may either like their job or hate it, or be somewhere in between, but they have this underlying feeling that they should be doing something else, more suited to who they are, where their true strengths lie, and what they most enjoy.

They look at their current career and, to steal a line from 'Once in a lifetime' by Talking Heads, they think to themselves, "Well, how did I get here?" Many people simply land in a particular career without much thought or planning, and suddenly wonder one day whether it's too late to change.

Changing careers is never easy because, in many cases, employers tend to view workers as specialists and don't offer the opportunity to try something new. An accountant may be overlooked for a job in marketing and a marketer may be overlooked for a job in accounting, even though they may be better suited to the new role than the one they're currently in.

You may decide that you want to leave corporate life behind altogether and pursue a career which is more aligned with your personal interests. You may even want to run your own business.To make such a decision requires an assessment of your personal circumstances - can you afford it financially to make this change into the unknown, and have you considered what you'll do if this new career doesn't work out?

Over the years, I have advised many disillusioned people about how to go about assessing their next career step. The simplest advice I have ever offered them is to start by taking a sheet of paper and dividing it into 3 columns. The first column should be headed, 'What am I good at?', the second column, 'What do I enjoy doing?' and the third column, 'What jobs enable me to do what I enjoy, and do it well?' This can be a very enlightening process, as it confronts you to put your thoughts down on paper and make an informed decision about what you really want to do with your career. It does take some navel gazing, followed by solid research, but the reward is worth the effort.

It confronts you to put your thoughts down on paper and make an informed decision.

If you decide that corporate life is your preferred option, but you're not satisfied with your current role, then it's time to design your next job. For a moment, imagine being in the movie industry and being able to write your own movie script, knowing that you're the central character and that when the movie is made, you're the one playing the lead role.

Designing your own job is no different (if you can forget about the fortune and fame for a minute) - it's just a matter of finding someone willing to fund it and help make it happen. When I counsel job seekers on how to design their next job, I liken it to a movie script, and suggest they break it up into 3 sections: Role, Company/Industry, and Remuneration.

Here is an example of a job design template that I've seen provide clarity to many a frustrated job seeker and set them on a path to finding a job that they're good at and enjoy doing.

First, let's look at the role

- What is the role? (what will you be doing?)
- Where is it based?
- What geographical coverage does the role have?
- Where does it fit into the organisation's structure?
- Who will you report to and where is that person based? What is this person's management style?

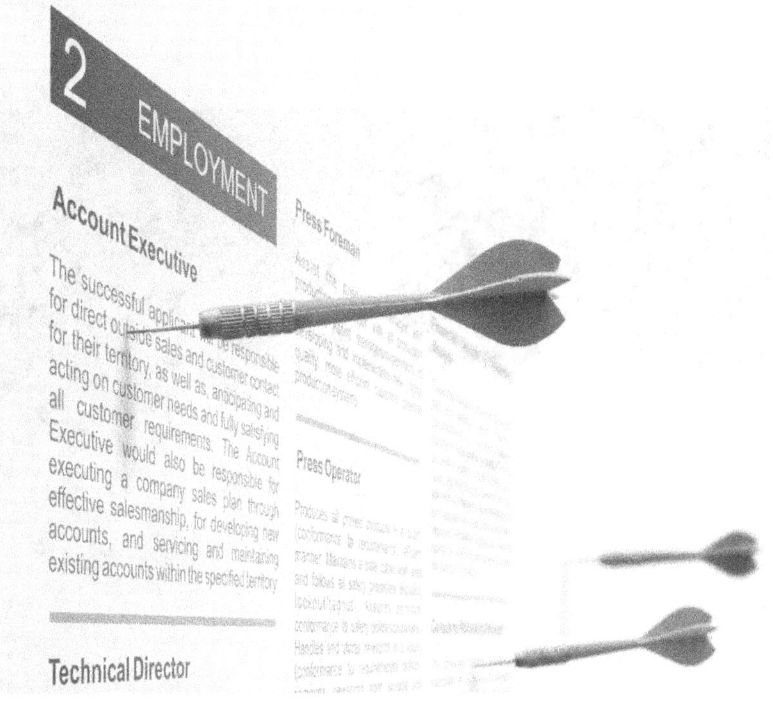

- Who reports to you and where are they based? Who reports to them?
- What are the Key Performance Indicators (KPIs) you'll be measured against?
- What impact will you make in the role?
- What do you want to be famous for in the organisation?
- What will be your next role in the organisation - will it be a vertical move within the function, taking on a new function, or combining your function with other functions?
- Who do you expect to predominantly deal with internally and externally?
- How much and how often will you travel?
- What will you do in your 1st month?
- What profile will you seek to build internally and externally?

Company/Industry

- What industry is the company in, or is it a conglomerate, comprising companies in various industries, like General Electric? What appeals to you about this industry?
- Is it a public or private company?

- Where is its head office based?
- How would you describe the organisation's culture?
- Where is the company/industry in terms of its evolution?

Remuneration

- What will you be paid and how will it be packaged - what portion is at risk, in terms of bonus, stock options, etc?

Taking control of what you want to do with your career should provide the challenges, job satisfaction and rewards that you're looking for.

What are you doing and are you happy doing it?

People who simply let their career happen to them, are the ones who can become disillusioned. It's like going on a road trip without a map and coming to a cross road - with no information to guide you, you may decide to turn left and after driving for 100 miles, you come to a dead end in the desert. If you had taken the time to plan your road trip and decide on your destination, based on what you most enjoy doing, then you would have known to turn right at the cross road and 5 miles later, you'd be sitting on the beach!

In closing this lesson, I encourage you to take a good look at your current career. What are you doing and are you happy doing it? If you're happy with the answer, congratulations, you're on the right path - if you're not happy with the answer, put this lesson into practice and get yourself on the right path - it's never too late.

LESSON 13

How do you hire the right staff?

How do you hire the right staff? You're right, it's not an easy exercise, whether you're hiring someone to flip burgers or to run a company. The cost of hiring the wrong staff can be a very expensive and damaging exercise, not just financially, but to the business' credibility and company morale.

In this lesson, you'll learn how to formalise the process of hiring staff and the importance of following that process every time in order to minimise, if not eradicate, the chances of hiring the wrong person. I remember being interviewed on CNBC in 1997 on this exact topic, and the information I shared then hasn't changed from what I'm sharing vvith you today.

Let's start at the point when you know there's a need to hire a new staff member. The first task is to ensure that you fully understand the job that you're hiring for.

Start by asking yourself, "What has to be achieved in this job?" These are known as Key Result Areas, or KRAs. Once these have been established, the next step is to identify the key tasks, which are necessary for these results to be achieved. Once you know what needs to be achieved and what the staff member needs to do to achieve them, you can then decide on the Key Performance Indicators, or KPIs, which shows how the results will be measured. You now have a sufficient foundation on which to build an accurate job profile, which can be recruited for.

Let's look at an example of identifying KRAs, key tasks, and KPIs for a particular job, in this case an Accounting Manager. Here are a number of KRAs:

1. Completion of monthly accounts within 3 days of month end, compared with 7 days currently: Deadline - end of financial year
2. Provide meaningful analysis of financial information to senior management, with a view to improving the P&L by 10% by the end of the next financial year
3. Implementation of Oracle financial system by the end of the financial year
4. Hire 3 new people for Accounting team by end of financial year

You can see that the 4 KRAs are specific results that the company wants to see achieved. Let's focus on the first KRA and establish the key tasks that need to be undertaken to ensure that a 3 day close after month end is achieved:

1. Gain co-operation from other departments to submit their financial data (eg; sales figures, inventory levels) to the Accounting department by an agreed deadline
2. Streamline accounting procedures, including the removal of unnecessary process duplication
3. Encourage accounting staff to rethink how they manage their 'link in the chain' with a view to improving efficiency
4. Smooth implementation of Oracle system

Okay, we've established a number of key tasks that the Accounting Manager will need to undertake if the KRAs are to be achieved. Next question is, how do we measure the results? The KPIs in this case are fairly obvious:

1. Accurate monthly accounts are completed within 3 days of month end
2. P&L improved with positive feedback from senior management
3. Oracle system is implemented on time and on budget
4. 3 new staff have joined the Accounting team

Now that you know what the most important aspects of the role are, you can prepare the job description, encompassing all of the responsibilities of the role. Once you have that finished, you then need to ask yourself about the kind of person you think will be most successful in the role.

Skills, knowledge, and attributes, otherwise known as competencies.

Regardless of what type of role you are hiring for, in all cases, you are trying to find the person with the best combination of skills, knowledge, and attributes, otherwise known as competencies. If we look at the Accounting Manager position again, examples of skills could be the ability to use Microsoft Excel and the ability to meet deadlines through effective planning.

Examples of knowledge could be 5 years of experience using the same Oracle financial software that you're looking to implement in the coming year, or a particular academic qualification. Examples of attributes could be a willingness to work long hours and weekends to achieve the 3 day accounts deadline at month end, or the desire to partner with other departments to bring more meaning to the monthly figures, through better interpretation and teamwork. Attributes reflect the person's needs, values and interests, and identify whether they have the attitude required to succeed in the job and the company's culture.

Once you have developed the competency profile of the person you think will best succeed, the next step is to develop a set of interview questions, designed to find out which candidates have the competencies you're looking for, and which ones don't. Many organisations around the world use a method of interviewing, simply called competency based interviewing.This method uses open ended questions, starting with words such as how, what, when, where, which, why, or who.

These questions can't be answered with a simple yes or no. The key objective is to ask questions which require the candidate to talk about what they have actually done in a particular situation, rather than what they would do. This is an important distinction to make, because you are looking for facts, not opinions. Do you see the difference here?

It is all about what the candidate has actually done, not what they would do.

Let's go back to the Accounting Manager role and the 3rd KRA we listed, implementation of an Oracle financial system. An interview question you may want to ask is, "Tell me about the Oracle implementation project you were a part of in your current company. What was your role, what did you do, and what was the result?" The candidate will then have to provide you with a factual account of how he/she used that exact competency and what success was achieved. You must be attentive when listening to the answer, as some candidates may say "We did this…", but you want to know what the candidate did themselves. It is all about what the candidate has actually done, not what they would do.

By using these kinds of questions, you want the candidate to provide you with what's commonly known as a STAR. This stands for

Situation, Task, Action and Result, and such answers offer you an insight into the candidate's past behaviour, which can be used as a predictor of future behaviour. These questions can have negative as well as positive connotations. A negative oriented question to ask the candidate may be, "Tell me about a time at your current company, where you had conflict with another member of staff. What did you do and what was the result?" Asking for these specific examples will allow you to discover whether the candidate has done the things that you'll need them to do successfully in your role.

Once you have advertised the role and are ready to start interviewing a list of candidates, a good idea is to draw a grid on a sheet of paper, with each candidate's name across the top and each of the competencies down the side. Ask each candidate exactly the same questions and tick or cross each relevant box, so at the end of the interview process, you can easily measure which candidate has the combination of competencies that you're looking for. You won't overlook or misinterpret any important information, you won't rush your decision, and you'll be objective. The best combination of these competencies should result in maximum performance, satisfaction, productivity and tenure.

You won't rush your decision, and you'll be objective.

What I've been talking about in this lesson, I like to call the 'science' part of the process, the part ruled by your head. I do also recommend though, that you add a little bit of 'art' to that process, the part ruled by your heart.The combination of head and heart should ensure that not only does your head tell you that this person is well qualified for the role, but your heart tells you that you like them as well and believe that they'll blend in with your company culture very easily.

Hiring staff in a hurry, basing your decision on gut instinct, and not having a structured platform for preparing the job profile, interview questions, and candidate assessment, only increases the risk of getting it wrong, so make every effort to do your homework, plan your approach, and enjoy the rewards. Over the years, I have advised interviewers to take this structured approach to their interview process to help decrease the risk of hiring the wrong person.

LESSON 14

Self-Marketing: How do you keep yourself in the spotlight?

Have you ever sat back and wondered how someone you've worked closely with, suddenly received a promotion, or got head-hunted to join a new company in a larger and more important role? What about someone you started with at the same time, but within 5 years, they have flown 3 levels above you?

Going through this experience can be pretty demoralising and frustrating, especially if you feel that it should be you receiving the accolades, instead of continually being overlooked. You may even feel resentment, and such negative energy isn't much use to anyone.

So, how do you become the person who receives the promotion or call from a head-hunter? So much of this has to do with what I call 'self-marketing', or in other words, your ability to stay in the spotlight, keep blinking on the radars of those people who can help guide your future, and remaining current, rather than stagnant.

This lesson focuses on some of the key elements of self-marketing, and I recommend that you consider each of them, as a way to enhance the probability that you will receive the next promotion or call from a head-hunter.

The first element I want to talk about is:

Volunteering for project teams linked to high profile projects

If you know that an important project is coming up, and you feel that you have the relevant competencies to make a vital contribution, then put your hand up for consideration. The project could be the implementation of a new computer system, the company's relocation to new offices, or the integration of your company with a merger partner. Now, it's obvious that all of these projects are of varying scale and will require people with different competency profiles, so you need to be confident that you can deliver, before volunteering to join the project team.

I'd like to use a good friend of mine as an example, to illustrate how this can work in your favour. In early 1994, he had been working in the recruitment industry for 4 months, and one morning, he was invited to a meeting in the boardroom. At the meeting were the State Managing Director, Administration Manager, and 5 Business Unit Managers. He was the only non-management person at the meeting and started to worry a little, as to why he had been asked to meet with such a group. The State Managing Director then explained that the company's head office had suggested to him that this office host the company's annual conference in the coming November - the first time that the conference would not be hosted by head office.

Consider what contribution you can make.

All present at the meeting were invited to form the project team and put the whole event together. My friend looked around the room and immediately realised that this was a team he wanted to succeed with. The group split up into 2 person teams to each focus on key components, and met once a week to discuss progress. The team environment was wonderful and it was a great learning experience being with such positive high achievers. The conference was a huge success and the joint CEOs paid tribute to the group's leadership, creativity, dedication, high standards, attention to detail and team dynamic.

My friend looks back on that experience as so important to his development at the company. The exposure to senior management was amazing and the success of the conference placed him under a positive spotlight.

Three years later, he was sent overseas to set up a new Asian operation in Hong Kong, and when he was briefed by one of the joint CEOs on why he was asked to relocate, the CEO reflected on the role my friend had played on the conference project team, saying that the character traits he showed then, had continued throughout the last 3 years and made him both a worthy candidate and a great asset to the business.

You might think that the project I've used in this example isn't exactly life changing, but it was for my friend, as it enabled him to show what he could achieve to the people who had the power to guide his future. All I can advise, is to consider what contribution you can make to important and high profile future projects, and as long as the project won't have a negative impact on your current workload, then put up your hand.

The second element of self-marketing is:

Being open to relocation

This may not be relevant to all of you, but it will be relevant to a lot of you. Let me share another example with you. From 1994 to 1997, I recruited dozens of 22-25 year old Accountants for a global industrial corporation. This corporation had the most highly esteemed finance development program in the industry and therefore, they were extremely fussy about who they hired to join the program.

These 22-25 year olds all had brilliant grades in their high school and university degrees, and were high achievers in their employment. They were also successful in their personal lives, with achievements in music, sports, community services, etc.

One of the most important characteristics that the corporation was looking for from these candidates was a willingness to relocate.

They had operations all over the world and preferred to grow their Accountants, by sending them to a new role every 3-4 years, in a different part of the business and in a different location. I met some of their staff, who had worked in the USA, Chile, Australia and Japan, within 15 years. As a new opportunity became available, the corporation would assess who they thought was ready for a move, then canvass the idea with the individual, and make it happen. These people continued to climb the ladder and their expertise grew exponentially.

Over time, those who became reluctant to relocate were overlooked for new opportunities and promotion - in other words, they began to stagnate, rather than grow and develop, and ultimately were the ones who left the corporation.

> **These people continued to climb the ladder and their expertise grew exponentially.**

I'm not saying that in general, if you don't relocate you won't succeed, however, many larger companies around the world, reward staff who are willing to take a chance and develop themselves and others in unfamiliar surroundings. Many Fortune 500 CEOs in the US have a track record of working in many countries, across a number of continents, rather than spending their entire career in the US.

It really does depend on the size of company that you're working for as to whether there will ever be a need for you to relocate, but always remember that you may be made more and better offers, if you're willing to move for the good of the company.

Now for the third element of self-marketing and that is:

Being seen as an industry expert

This is probably quite an obvious idea, however, it is amazing how many people don't promote themselves publicly, to enhance their reputation and marketability. Some people simply don't want a public profile, but others do and are just reluctant to take the first step.

There are a number of ways to develop a public profile as an industry expert. These include:

- Writing articles for industry magazines and newsletters, both offline and online
- Being interviewed by journalists from newspapers, magazines, television, radio, podcasts, etc
- Speaking at industry seminars, professional associations, conferences, alumni presentations
- Writing a book, an industry paper, or even a blog

Over the years, I have seen people maintain a healthy public profile as industry experts, simply by being 'go to' people for the media, when a particular event needs commenting on. Whether you're an economist offering your views on interest rates and inflation data, or a psychologist talking about stress in the work place, the broader community will see you as an expert and your value will increase as a result.

The barrier to most people not pursuing a public profile is self-confidence. People think to themselves, “Why would the public want to hear what I have to say?” or “What if I make a fool of myself?” and it’s this fear and lack of confidence that is hard to overcome, until you actually make the effort and realise that it’s not that hard. The key is to choose a subject that you know well enough so that you’re seen as being credible by your audience.

Whether you’re a banker, engineer, management consultant, architect, teacher, nurse, electrician, sales executive, hairdresser, actor, or professional sports person, there will be a subject that you know well enough to offer your perspectives to the public in some format. Simply think about the topic, think about your target audience, and channel your approach in that direction.

The fourth and final element of self-marketing that I want to talk about in this lesson is:

Being involved in inductee training

If you work for a company that offers induction training for new employees, then you can really improve your profile internally by offering to conduct part of the induction program. That way, you spend time with new staff, pass on valuable knowledge to them, and ultimately impress management with your initiative and leadership.

I'd like to share an example of this with you. When I worked with a leading executive search firm in Hong Kong in the late 1990s, I remember one of our personal assistants (PA), who was quite shy and unassuming, but did her job as well as any other PA in the company, and we employed at least 20 at the time. She was asked by management to conduct a section of the new induction program, not for new PAs, but for new recruitment consultants.

The section was about policies and procedures for the working relationship between consultants and their PAs and systems that had to be followed for ISO 9002 quality accreditation, which was a global quality standard that the company had to comply with.

This PA was nervous and very apprehensive about accepting the task, but with continued encouragement, she took on the challenge.

Self-marketing is driven by you, your energy, commitment and confidence.

I'm very happy to tell you that she excelled in the role, her confidence grew, as did her reputation within the company, and within a year, she was promoted to Office Manager, with total responsibility for the 20 or so PAs in the company. She simply never knew she had it in her, until she took the risk to find out. It's a great story and she's a great lady.

As an addition to your participation in inductee training, you may want to nominate yourself as a 'buddy', which we talked about in Lesson 9. Each new employee is assigned a buddy, who they can go to at any time during their settling in period with the company, to seek advice, share ideas or simply confide in. If you feel that you're a person who reflects the company's values and possesses the core competencies that the new employee will ultimately need to be a successful contributor, then you should definitely offer your services as a 'buddy'. I'm confident that this will do wonders for your profile.

Self-marketing is driven by you, your energy, commitment and confidence. Whether you want to increase your visibility within your company or on a larger scale within the broader community, it's up to you to step into the traffic, put your hand up, and offer something that people will benefit from.This should always lead to a win-win situation, for you and the people you've connected with.

LESSON 15

How do you manage your own performance and what should you expect in your performance review?

You go to work and you do your job. You probably think you're doing a good job, but how do you really know? You may receive the odd piece of positive or negative feedback from your boss, but is that enough for you to know whether or not you're ultimately succeeding or failing in your role and how highly valued you are by the company?

How your performance is assessed will obviously depend on the company that you join and their approach to performance assessment. Some companies will take an unscientific approach, and simply make a once a year subjective judgement, usually at salary review time, based on minimal if any data. It could be based purely on the assessor's feelings about you, and not provide an objective basis for further discussion.

Other companies utilise various tools to help them assess the performance of their staff, which then helps them structure each staff member's future, in terms of training & development, salary & bonus, promotion, and in negative cases, actual termination from the company. Many of these tools still require subjective opinion from the assessors, however the overall assessment comes from a much more rational than emotional perspective.

One commonly used assessment tool is 360° feedback, which generally involves up to 12 colleagues providing feedback on your performance across a number of criterion in a survey format. To produce a full 360° result, the people asked to provide feedback will include your boss, your peers, your staff and your customers. The criterion will probably involve such things as communication skills, quality, meeting deadlines, helping others, being proactive, sharing information, and team orientation. This kind of feedback requires subjective evaluation, but will show you exactly how you are being perceived across the board.

I don't think that 360° feedback should be used in isolation as a performance review, as it's based on people's opinions rather than exact and trackable data, but it's very useful in the overall assessment process.

This kind of feedback requires subjective evaluation.

The best basis for producing accurate and effective performance review criteria is to first establish the key result areas or key performance indicators (KPIs) of the role. As we discussed in Lesson 13, by defining the most important elements of your role, you then know exactly what needs to be achieved and what doing a great job will look like. Some of the performance indicators will be trackable with actual data (for example, reaching 100% of your sales budget), whilst others won't be based on actual data (for example, you as an Accountant, trying to improve relations between the accounting and sales teams) and will require more subjective assessment.

From my experience, a successful strategy to employ for an effective and constructive performance review happens long before your actual review - it happens when you first start your new job. Just imagine that you are starting a new job and you want to do it well. You sit down with your new boss and the key performance indicators of the role are explained to you. You agree that you understand what needs to be achieved in order for you to succeed in the role, and then off you go.

It is this clarity that ensures that both you and your boss know what you need to achieve in order to receive a positive performance review and continue to progress in the company. When you have your actual review with your boss (reviews are usually held annually), you will discuss how you have performed against each of the KPIs and reasons why you have or haven't achieved each of them. It is important for your boss to hear your perspective on what has and hasn't gone well and why. From there, you may then work with your boss in choosing and agreeing upon appropriate KPIs for you to achieve in the next review period. Now that you're experienced in the role, your input is highly valuable in this process, because you have a much better idea of what you're capable of, but you'll also be held much more accountable.

A good next step in the review is to develop a SWOT analysis with your boss, which basically identifies your strengths, weaknesses, opportunities and threats. A strength may be your ability to close sales with clients, a weakness could be time management, an opportunity may be to expand your role to include managing staff, and a threat could be that your best client is relocating to the other side of the country. This SWOT analysis can then help your boss construct an appropriate training and development plan for you.

Now please forgive me for assuming that one of the best ways to motivate you to achieve the KPIs, is for your boss to link your bonus remuneration to them. There may be a provision for you to earn a 10% bonus at the end of the year if you achieve your KPIs, and because you've known this all year, you have been committed to succeeding. You may only achieve half of your KPIs and therefore receive a 5% bonus, but you appreciate the fact that your performance is linked to your reward.

Follow up periodically throughout the year to discuss progress.

Assuming that your review period is once a year, it is in the best interests of you and your boss to follow up periodically throughout the year to discuss progress and make any necessary adjustments, to ensure that you're on the right track. An agreed course of action and regular follow up are critical to all parties buying into the process and partnering for success.

Performance reviews don't need to be exclusive to your work. You may be an achievement oriented person and pride yourself on performing to the best of your ability in many aspects of your life. You may ask for feedback from your sports or fitness coach, your spouse, your friends or your parents. This process may not be as formal and structured as the review you do at work, however you will probably appreciate another person's perspective apart from your own on how you're doing.

Make the effort to manage your own performance. Just say one of your identified weaknesses is time management; you may notice that you're a poor time manager, not just at work but in general. You might then decide to make becoming a better time manager your number one life goal for the year, and doing simple things like using a daily planner and a to do list will help you achieve that goal.

That's just one example of keeping track of your progress. If there is anything you want to improve on, simply set some performance indicators and keep track of your progress. You may want to run your first marathon under 4 hours. In order to achieve this, you may need to improve your diet, heart rate, muscle flexibility, and stamina. An appropriate course of action would be to prepare a training log, and as you continue to train, you can review your progress and make any necessary adjustments to your training, to keep you on track for that sub-4 hour marathon.

You can see that performance reviews and performance management are just as applicable to your personal life as they are to your work, and are an excellent way to help you to be the person you want to be.

This brings the 15th and final lesson to a close and I want to thank you for taking this journey with me. I'm sure you agree that the 15 lessons we have shared together, will continue to help you throughout your career, as an employee, as an employer, and as a person.

I look forward to keeping in touch and wish you continued success and happiness in your personal and professional life.

Brian Moore is the founder and creator of the Career Management Toolkit. He has specialised in executive recruitment and career management since the early 1990s.

Learn more at

www.BrianMooreExecutiveSearch.com

"This is an excellent read worth referring to, when facing career decisions, or a deadlock at work, or when you're forced to rethink your career."

Brian is a veteran in his field, not only as a recruitment consultant, but also as a career coach. To me, his advice has been very pragmatic, precise and has many times guided me through different stages of career movement. These 15 lessons cover a very wide range of areas that we all face in our working life at different times, and have summarized most of the candid and useful advice he has given me for the last 10 years I've known him as a friend and a coach.

EDMOND LAU (HONG KONG)

"Whether you are looking for a job now or not, the Career Management Toolkit is a must read. I highly recommend it."

This was the first time in my career that I had to commence a search for a new job. I have held strategic positions within the financial services industry in all the major centers: New York, London, Tokyo and Hong Kong. I was not sure where to start.

I met Brian in the mid 1990s in Hong Kong during one of my overseas assignments. Brian and I established a very good relationship and we have kept in touch over the years. As I was launching my search, Brian was one of the first calls that I made. In addition to support and advice, Brian offered me his Career Management Toolkit. There are many guides available, but after reading the toolkit a few times, there were many insightful concepts that really made sense to me. It is very well written and I have picked it up on a number of occasions to read specific sections.

Recently, I received an offer from a financial institution and utilized Lesson 1 - The 10 Ps of choosing the right job to make my decision. This toolkit does not stop here. It is extremely useful as one starts a new job. The first few months are critical and there are sections in the toolkit that will assist in the transition.

Whether you are looking for a job now or not, the Career Management Toolkit is a must read. I highly recommend it.

MARK COHEN (USA)

Special Offer

Let's not end our relationship here.

I want to continue to add value to your ongoing career success and satisfaction, so simply send an email to

Offer@CareerManagementToolkit.com

and you'll receive a presentation I made earlier this year, titled:

'The importance of life long career planning, how to develop an ongoing career plan & useful career planning tools.'

On a separate note, if you would like professional help to prepare your resume, I'd be happy to help you. Contact me at:

Brian@BrianMooreExecutiveSearch.com

or visit:

www.BrianMooreExecutiveSearch.com

and click the link under 'Are you a C-Suite job seeker?', titled 'Does your resume need updating?'

Be your best and love your life.
Brian

BRIAN MOORE

Brian Moore International Pte Ltd

Career Management Toolkit is the brainchild and passion of Brian Moore. Brian joined the executive recruitment and career management industry in 1993, recruiting Finance Directors and CFOs for a major listed global recruitment group, before transferring to the company's Hong Kong office in early 1997. Brian created, built and led two North Asian recruitment businesses, which continued to grow profitably until late 1999, when he decided to follow his dream.

Brian launched his own company, Brian Moore International (BMI) in late 1999, initially focusing on working as a personal agent for job seekers around the world. He's been described by many as the 'Jerry Maguire' of the executive recruitment industry, and has represented executives from over 20 countries, across multiple industries and disciplines.

Since founding BMI, Brian has successfully built the business across **6 key offerings**:

- C-Suite Executive Search
- Career Management Toolkit
- Career Transition Management
- Executive CV Preparation
- HR Services (including Outplacement)
- Speaking Engagements

Brian created the **Career Management Toolkit** to share the knowledge and expertise that he has accumulated throughout his career, with the aim to help the global workforce make better and more informed career decisions.

Brian has appeared as a career management expert on CNBC television in Asia and ABC radio in Australia. He has also been profiled in both CFO Asia and CFO Innovation magazines in Hong Kong and by a prominent Australian daily newspaper. He has presented to high school and university students, at industry conferences and to corporate executives on topics including the importance of life long career planning, how to develop an ongoing career plan & useful career planning tools.

When not working, Brian spends valuable time with his wife, daughter, son and pet Golden Retriever. He is an avid runner and tennis player, with a huge passion for music.

Find more at:

BrianMooreExecutiveSearch.com
CareerManagementToolkit.com
twitter.com/better_career
facebook.com/CareerManagementToolkit

www.ingramcontent.com/pod-product-compliance
Lightning Source LLC
LaVergne TN
LVHW020642100826
845148LV00012B/2305

* 9 7 8 0 6 4 6 5 2 5 0 4 4 *